Cracking the Communication Code

Nonviolent Communication

by 42 Key Differentiations

Liv Larsson & Katarina Hoffmann

www.friareliv.se

Cracking the Communication Code by Liv Larsson & Katarina Hoffmann

Friare Liv
Mjösjölidvägen 477
946 40 Svensbyn
Sweden
Phone: +46911- 24 11 44
info@friareliv.se
www.friareliv.se

Author: Liv Larsson & Katarina Hoffmann
Translation: Katarina Hoffmann www.13steg.se
Editor: Liv Larsson
Layout: Kay Rung
Cover and illustrations: Vilhelm PH Nilsson: vilhelm@uppsalanaturbete.se

ISBN:978-91-87489-31-0

Content

Quick Guide

If you would like to read about Key Differentiations within a special area, this quick guide will make it easier to find what you are looking for.

Key Differentiations Concerning the Four NVC-components (Observations, Feelings, Needs and Requests)

1. "Observations" versus "Evaluations".
2. "Feelings" versus "Thoughts".
3. "Needs" versus "Strategies".
4. "Vague Requests" versus "Clear, Doable Requests".
5. "To Request what I do want" versus "To Request what I do not want.
6. "Request" versus "Demand".

Key Differentiations Concerning "Jackals" and "Giraffes"

7. "Classical Giraffe" versus "Idiomatic Giraffe".
8. "Living Giraffe" versus "Doing Giraffe".
9. "Jackal Honesty" versus "Giraffe Honesty".
10. "Screaming in Jackal" versus "Screaming in Giraffe".
11. "No in Jackal" versus "No in Giraffe".
12. "Saying 'I am sorry' in Giraffe" versus "Saying 'I am sorry' in Jackal".

Key Differentiations Concerning Honesty

1. "Observations" versus "Evaluations".
2. "Feelings" versus "Thoughts".
3. "Needs" versus "Strategies".
4. "Vague Requests" versus "Clear, Doable Requests".
9. "Honesty in Giraffe" versus "Honesty in Jackal".
28. "Judgments Based on Right and Wrong"
    versus "Judgments based on Needs".
35. "Stimulus" versus "Cause".

Key Differentiations Concerning Empathy

13. "Empathy Focusing on Content" versus
    "Empathy Focusing on Process".
14. "Empathy Focusing on Needs" versus
    "Empathy Focusing on Unmet Needs".
15. "Stating" versus "Guessing".
16. "Guessing Intellectually" versus "Guessing Empathically".
17. "Sympathy" versus "Empathy".
18. "Advice" versus "Empathy".
19. "Listen Empathically" versus "Consoling".
20. "Mourning" versus "Giving up".
21. "Self-empathy" versus "Self-pity".
22. "Self-empathy" versus "Acting out Your Feelings".

Key Differentiations Concerning Self-empathy

13. "Empathy Focusing on Content" versus
    "Empathy Focusing on Process".
17. "Sympathy" versus "Empathy".
20. "Mourning" versus "Giving up".
21. "Self-empathy" versus "Self-pity".

22. "Self-empathy" versus "Acting out Your Feelings".

Key Differentiations Concerning Power

23. "Systems Based on Domination" versus "Need-based Systems".
24. "Power With" versus "Power Over".
25. "Fear of Authorities" versus "Respect for Authorities".
26. "Obedience" versus "Self Discipline".
27. "Protective use of force" versus "Punitive use of force".
28. "Judgments Based on Right and Wrong" versus "Judgments Based on Needs".
29. "Punishments" versus "Consequences".
30. "Weakness" versus "Vulnerability".
31. "Inner Motivation" versus "External Motivation".
32. "Freedom of Choice" versus "Dependence".
33. "Dependence or Independence" versus "Interdependence".
34. "Appreciation" versus "Approval".

Other

35. "Stimulus" versus "Cause".
36. "Compromise" versus "Shift".
37. "Acts that serve life" versus "Acts that distance us from life".
38. "Demand" versus "Being Firm".
39. "Love as a Feeling" versus "Love as a Need".
40. "Natural" versus "Habitual".
41. "Accomplish" versus "Create".
42. "Open Questions" versus "Closed Questions".

Key Differentiations

For Deeper Understanding of Nonviolent Communication

We have written this book to highlight some concepts in Nonviolent Communication (NVC), that differ from concepts we are accustomed to using in our everyday communication; concepts that we hope will clarify some of the essential differences between NVC and our accustomed way to communicate.

We call those differences "Key Differentiations" and in this book we describe a selection of them. We hope that you, when you explore these differences, will discover new ways to think and communicate.

With the help of the Key Differentiations we present here, you can decide when and how you want to use the four basic components of NVC – observations, feelings, needs and requests.

Hopefully the differentiations will help you to clarify the choice you have in really listening in a way that connects you to yourself and others. In doing so you will find that your communication will become more open and free.

This book does not cover all aspects of NVC; instead we focus on the Key Differentiations, as they illustrate essential parts of our communication and the way we handle conflicts.Our guess is that when you deepen your awareness of them, you will have a source of inspiration to draw from whenever you want to find new ways to relate to people around you.

The Key Differentiations help us to explain a not so well known - or even unknown – concept, through a more familiar one. It is a lot easier to describe a tandem bicycle if we can start by describing how it differs from a regular bike, assuming a bike is an object the other person is familiar with. If we want to say something about the Japanese instrument koto, it is easier if we can start with a harp, dulcimer, or a Swedish keyed fiddle. We do not in this case claim to have categorized all stringed instruments as kotos, kanteles or keyed fiddles. We only describe the differences between them and we do not say anything about their quality. And we do not say that one is "right" and the other "wrong" or that one is better than the other. We just want to answer the question: "What's the difference?" Just the fact that the question is asked is for us as important as how we try to answer it.

"Jackals" and "Giraffes"

NVC is also called the "Giraffe language", because we sometimes use the symbols "Giraffe" and "Jackal" for pedagogical reasons[1]. In some countries other animals are used. Whatever animal used we do not want to paint a black picture of wolves or jackals or any other animal. On the contrary, we want to emphasize the valuable messages that are hidden behind what the "Jackal" tells us.

The "Giraffe" is used as a symbol for language which facilitates a more direct way to connect effectively. It also corresponds with the NVC position that we naturally want to contribute to each other, when we can do so out of free will.

The "Jackal" is used as a symbol for language that makes it challenging to connect. Sometimes we succeed, sometimes we do not. As many of us are used to thinking in terms of "right" and "wrong" we sadly get caught in thoughts that "Jackal language" is "wrong" and "Giraffe language" is "right". That is NOT our intention when using these symbols! Our intention is to clarify some of the Key Differentiations and thereby make it easier to explore and to learn new ways of communicating.[2]

---

1. We choose to write "Jackal" and "Giraffe" with capital letters and quotes to emphasize that it is the symbol and not the animal we are referring to.
2. Knowledge of Key Differentiations is one part in the certification process for people who want to be associated with CNVC (Center for Nonviolent Communication).

Key Differentiation 1

"Observations" versus "Evaluations"

"To observe without judging is the highest form of intelligence."
J. KRISHNAMURTI

When we can separate our observations from our interpretations we diminish the risk that others will hear us as being judgmental.

An **observation** is something we experience with our senses; seeing, hearing, sense of smell, taste and touch. We usually say that an observation is what a digital recorder captures.

Evaluations are conclusions we draw from what we observe. With the help of evaluations we describe the good or bad points of the person or occurrence we have observed. Usually evaluations form the basis for our judgment about something we experience; is it good, bad, normal or abnormal. Evaluations are like a review of a movie or recording we have observed.

If we watch a person rise from the sofa, walk towards the TV, grab it, walk to the opposite side of the room carrying the TV, and throw it out through a closed window, this is what a digital recorder can register. If we see something like this, it is likely that we, when telling about it, will add some evaluations like:
"He is absolutely crazy! He grabbed the TV and threw it out the window."

No one can tell from this information whether he is crazy or not, it is an evaluation. Perhaps the action he took is – in another evaluation – appropriate. He may have noticed smoke coming from the TV. In this case our evaluation might have been that he reacted boldly.

Another example is of a person donating 20 dollars to the account

of an orphanage, an act that can be interpreted as either generous or miserly, depending on our judgment of the person or of the amount given. If we are to tell someone about it we could say:

"She is so generous; even if she only has her pension to live on, she do-nated 20 dollars to the orphanage."

If the person is known as one of the wealthiest people in town, the same act, giving 20 dollars to the needy, could have been la-beled miserly. As a matter of fact we know nothing about the person or her finances. Perhaps she just wanted to pay off a bill and being careless – also an evaluation – deposited the money in the wrong account.

1

Reflection

Our inability to keep observations separate from evaluations may create or intensify enemy images. During the 2005 flood in New Orleans we heard a reporter reporting on people en-tering unattended grocery stores, looking for food, his comment was:

"They wanted to help their families and themselves to survive at any cost".

The people in these pictures he was referring to were all Cau-casians. When reporting from another part of the city he talked about the "*looting*" of shops. The people in these pictures were all of African american origin.

This kind of evaluation in reporting can both create and main-tain enemy images and strengthen our preconceived biases. In these cases we are not ourselves observing what actually happens or what someone is actually doing; we are using the information given to us to confirm images already established in our brain.

During my studies at the university we were subject to an "eye witness experiment". Its purpose was to shed light on how the images in our brain – usually called prejudices or preconceived ideas – affect what we think we see.

We were presented with a film sequence showing a car accident. One of the cars involved was a brand new Mercedes gliding noiselessly, the other a hot rod with a broken muffler.

The collision was - according to my interpretation – violent. After the show we were asked to fill out a form. Among the things they wanted us to estimate was the speed of the cars involved. We were also asked to tell who caused the accident according to the existing traffic regulations. All students were convinced that the hot rod was speeding; breaking the traffic rules and thereby caused the collision.

When we watched the film a second time we were all crestfallen – an interpretation – to see that the opposite was true ... the driver of the Mercedes was the speeding driver, the one who caused the collision.

Key Differentiation 2

"Thoughts" versus "Feelings"

We often find it challenging to listen to our feelings and to separate them from our thoughts. Someone said that the distance between the heart and the brain is the longest half-yard in the world.

Our **thoughts** are - among other things - the sense we make of our feelings and of the reasons for them. Those thoughts are shaped by the culture we grew up in, and the language we have learned. We imagine things and sometimes draw conclusions too prematurely. Sometimes we also add "information" to construct a reality that suits our feelings better.

Feelings, as we use the word, are reactions we experience in our body. Words for feelings are an attempt to name those bodily reactions. We consider feelings a bodily reaction sending us a signal as to whether our needs are met or not. Therefore feelings vary – often moment-by-moment – depending on the circumstances.[1] Sometimes we express a mixture of thoughts and feelings which make it difficult to connect with others and ourselves.

Reflection

If an oncoming car gets into "my lane" while overtaking a trailer, I might express my fear by crying out loud because I am terrified. A likely thought in this situation could be: "What a reckless driver."

When someone for the third time in a row is late for an appointment with me I might feel frustrated, and show it by pacing back and forth with tears of anger running down my cheeks. A possible thought might be: "He doesn't give a darn about me!"

If we mix our feelings and our thoughts we might end up saying something like this to the person: "I feel totally worthless because you just ignore me."

If we focus on our feelings we get a signal telling us what we need and we can act to meet that need. When we, on the other

---

1 You can read more in Nonviolent Communication, a language for life, by Marshall Rosenberg. Puddle Dancer Press. Chapter 3.

hand, focus on our thoughts, we easily get caught in anger or depression.

Not knowing how to separate thoughts from feelings can contribute to loss of connection with our needs. In this case there is a high risk that what we say will be heard as criticism and who wants to continue listening if we get accused of ignoring a person?

Our chance to be heard and to get what we need will increase if we focus on our feelings and not on our thoughts. If we focus on thoughts when, for example, a feeling of loneliness is alive in us, perhaps we just withdraw especially if we have internalized the thought that it is "courageous to stand alone" and a bad thing to be needy or dependent. If we on the other hand listen to the feeling of loneliness, we can discover that we have a need of support and community and see that there are many different ways for us to have that need met. The feeling will guide us to one or more needs that we all share.

2

Key Differentiation 3

"Needs" versus "Strategies"

3

When we talk about **needs** we have in mind the driving force we are born with that helps us act to sustain and develop life itself. Those needs are universal and by that we mean they are the same for every human being, independent of where in the world or in which culture she or he is born.

Strategies describe what we do in fact, or plan to do, in order to meet our universal needs - the different actions we take.

Connection to our needs - as well as to the actions we choose to meet them with - can improve the quality of our lives. But strategies can also cause conflicts between individuals and sometimes we also choose actions that are not in harmony with our planet.

An obvious difference between needs and strategies - the actions we take to get them met - is that needs are the same for everyone, whilst strategies are specific when it comes to who is doing what, how it is done and when it is done.

The words "need" and "needy" are in many languages used to describe not only universal needs – the vital needs we are born with – they are also used to denote actions we would rather call just strategies. In daily life many people use the word "need" if they want something to eat, intimacy, a new car, or a pay increase.

For us, food and intimacy are needs, whereas the new car and the pay increase are strategies or "acquired needs"; the opposite of "innate needs".

In NVC it is essential to be able to separate the needs from the strategies we use to meet them. Conflicts usually originate from the strategies we have chosen to meet our needs.

As soon as one or both parties in a conflict recognize the needs involved and separate them from the strategies they have used so far, it is easier for them to handle the conflict. Once we understand that the person with whom we experience a conflict is also "fighting" to meet needs, it is usually a lot easier to find strategies that will meet the needs of both parties involved - strategies where no one is giving in or giving up.

This is not to say that it is always the same needs one chooses to meet in the end as when the conflict started. A shift to another need might have occurred when the needs of the other person became known.

When we want to meet our needs and have figured out a strategy for what actions will do it for us, we usually put our thoughts into words and make a request, as concrete as possible, as to what we want to happen. We specify something that is doable, who we want to act, and when we want that action to take place.

As soon as we can differentiate needs from strategies – actions to meet them - it usually becomes obvious that a need can be met in several different ways. That insight gives us the freedom to act – not only to meet the need that is acute but also to take action to meet needs that might be important in the long run.

Reflection

When I was a child and felt lonely and bored, I often turned to my mother to beg for candy or cookies. What I actually needed was to experience more connection and purpose. To eat something sweet gave me a temporary relief but I was soon bored again. The feeling of loneliness returned, despite the candy. So already at a young age I got used to eating something as a strategy to handle my feelings.

3

This is something I have had to work on as a grown up. Instead of just falling into my old habit of eating something when my urge for sweets strikes me, nowadays I stop and connect to my needs. Even if it has been tough to change the pattern, it has also been rewarding to consciously embrace the idea of separating my needs from my strategies.

It took me a while to recognize that when I feel lonely or in need of community my need may be met by visiting a friend, making a phone call or writing a letter. If my need is for purposefulness it is usually healthier to go for a walk or read a book, rather than having something to eat.[1]

When we realize that our habitual actions don't fully serve our needs, we get a chance to change and develop. We can learn how to take our needs seriously and remember that our feelings are not something we want to run away from. Instead, we want to use them to get a better understanding of what is alive in us. As soon as we have that understanding we can choose strategies that contribute to us and fill our lives with joy and meaning.

---

1. Read more in Nonviolent Communication, a language of life, by Marshall Rosenberg. Puddle Dancer Press. Chapters 5 and 6.

Key Differentiation 4

"Vague Requests" versus "Clear, Doable Requests"

4

One of the four components in the NVC-process is making requests. Either we express our own requests – for connection or for some kind of action – or we listen to what others request from us.

When we talk about **vague requests**, we are referring to requests that are imprecise or expressed in a less explicit way.

The person expressing the request may be in contact with his or her feelings and needs and knows exactly what to ask for, yet he or she may formulate that wish in indirect ways.

The reason for this may be that we usually assume the other person understands what we need, without us ourselves being clear about it. This can turn into a more or less destructive game where the underlying assumption is something like: "If he or she hears this, they will understand what I want"; i.e. is a "mind reader".

A clear, doable request includes what we wish to happen or hear someone say. The request is clear if it states whom we want to do what and when. And it is doable if we state – as precisely as possible – what we want someone to do or say rather than what we want them not to do.[1]

---

1. See also Key Differentiation 6.

We believe many of the irritating situations and conflicts we experience in our daily life could have developed differently – or be avoided all together – if we more frequently paid attention to how we make our requests. For instance, stains of toothpaste in the wash basin or empty toilet paper tubes on the floor, not to mention "no toilet paper at all, might irritate us every morning. If we just express that we don't like starting the day with these annoying things, without saying what changes we would like to see, we risk being continually irritated.

When we don't ask clearly for what we want, but only tell others what irritates us or what "someone" ought to do, it makes it more difficult for us to get what we want; especially if that "someone" also gets irritated and defensively fights back. This will make it even harder to get what we wish for.

One example we often present in our workshops is the "garbage war" or "whose responsibility is it to take out the garbage and how often." We comment to the family at large, "Well, I notice the garbage bag is full again!", and then wait in suspense to see how long it will take for someone to take the responsibility of taking it out. We have always done it in the past and are irritated that no one else seems to be bothered by the smell. But we wait in vain; everyone else in the family seems to be as surprised as we are that the bag hasn't walked out on its own...

This is an example of a vague request having been made. It is more likely we will end the "war" if we can formulate a doable request. Something like:

4

I feel extremely irritated when I see the trash bag full again. I have a need for order and for cooperation around keeping our place nice and tidy. Are you willing – as the last thing you do before going to bed at night – to replace and put the full bag in the garbage can. Would it be OK for you to try this for a week?

Quite a lot of words perhaps, but hopefully we only have to say them once. At the same time we want to remind you that regardless of what kind of request we make - clear or vague – there is no guarantee that the other person will act according to our request. He or she has a free choice and perhaps will say "no" to one request and "yes" to something else. If we in the case of a "no" choose to punish him or her for this response, for example by putting a guilt trip on them, what we have asked for was not a request, but a demand.

Correspondingly we miss many chances to experience care and community, because we do not know how or what to ask for, in order to meet those needs. Many of us live with the idea that "if he or she just loved me deeply enough, they would understand what I need," a perception that is not very likely to get our needs met.[2]

---

2. Read more in Nonviolent Communication, a language of life, by Marshall Rosenberg. Puddle Dancer Press. Chapters 5 and 6.

Reflection

*D*o *you want to sit there?"* my friend asked and I answered: *"Yes, this is fine."*

His concern was heart-warming. But after some small talk I discovered it was more and more difficult to connect with him. His answers were unusually sharp and brief and after a while I asked him what was going on. He glared at me and said:
"You just care about yourself!"

I was flabbergasted and asked:
"What do you mean?"

He said:
"I could really use a rest."

I probably looked as the very picture of bewilderment and he made himself clearer:
"Yes, I was hoping for a brief nap."

After some gentle coaxing I realized that he, with his first question to me, actually had wanted me to move. He, himself, wanted to sit where he could lean his head against the wall and rest for a while. It was good for me to realize what was alive in him, as I know how easily enemy images can grow in us when needs are not met. He had, like so many of us, learned to hide his wishes in faintly outlined questions. His needs could have been met much easier had he started by saying:
"I'd love to rest for a while is it OK for you to change seats with me?

Key Differentiation 5

"To Request what I do want" versus "To Request what I do not want."

5

When we make a **request and ask for what we *do* want,** we formulate our request as something that is doable. If we also make clear which need, or needs, will be met if the other person chooses to comply with our request, chances are increased he or she will feel motivated to contribute to our needs.

When we **request what we do *not* want** we are telling someone else or ourselves what we want to stop being done for right now, to meet our needs.

We use two examples to illustrate the difference:

Example 1:
"I really long for company and wonder if you are willing to check your calendar, to see if we can make plans for three evenings this week for the whole family to meet?"

Compared to:
"I don't want you to work as much as you do."

Example 2:
"I really need some peace and quiet. Are you willing to use your headset when you listen to music the next half hour?"

Compared to:
"I really need some peace and quiet, so I'd like it if you didn't listen to the radio now."

Reflection

When we ask someone – ourselves included – *not* to do a specific thing; *not* to eat more, *not* to sit by the computer the entire evening or *not* to work so much, it is less likely the result will be to our satisfaction than if we ask for what we *do want* to see happen.

5

Through the years I have noticed how often we formulate our requests "in the negative". We tell what we *don't* want to see happen or what we *don't* want someone to say or do.

The above mentioned examples are not unusual. I myself asked my partner not to work as much as he did, whereupon he went to Spain to play golf with his buddies. When I asked my son not to listen to the radio, he turned on the TV instead. And how many times have I asked myself not to eat more calories than I burn, in order not to become ill, not to drag those extra kilos around, and yet I still constantly gained weight.

The last time I caught myself in this trap, I was in a conversation with a five-year-old. He said:

"Tilde is so stupid".

"You know", I responded *"I don't want you to say that about her"*; whereupon he immediately corrected himself and said it was Alex who was the stupid one.

Key Differentiation 6

"Request" versus "Demand"

When others hear demands from us they see only two possibilities: Submission or rebellion.

MARSHALL B. ROSENBERG.[1]

6

When we make a **request** we ask someone to do something only if they are willing. Their free will is of vital importance. If the person says "no" we may want to alter our request.

A request is composed of information about who we want to do what and when plus which of our needs would be met and how it would make us feel.

When we **demand** we focus on what we want to happen. We express who we *want* to do what, how and when by promising rewards or by using threats. When we demand we are usually stuck on the idea, that our needs can only be met in a certain way.

The difference between demands and requests becomes obvious when we ask how we will react, if the other person says "no". If it is a demand we will feel like punishing the person for not choosing to do as we say. If on the other hand we get a "no" when we make a request, the dialog will continue. Maybe we change our strategy when we hear what the other person says "yes" to as he or she says "no" to our request. We may find other ways to get our needs met. We may still experience feelings of grief or disappointment that we did not get our way, but we are fully aware, that our feelings are not caused by the other person. Our feelings are caused by needs we have and long to see met.

1. Rosenberg, Marshall (2003) Nonviolent Communication, a language of life. PuddleDancer Press.

When we make demands and use words like *should* and *must*, others will most likely respond by rebelling. I once had an appointment at a garage to get my car serviced, but discovered, well in advance, that I could not bring my car in at the prearranged date. I called the garage several times, but no one answered the phone or called me back. Some days later I received a letter with information about where to put the keys and the service book when I brought in the car.

6

When I saw the letter and the sender I thought "now I'll inform them that I want to change the date for the service, since I can't do without the car that day." But when I opened it I immediately caught sight of the sentence:

"If the time is not okay you MUST inform us at once. We will charge you 50 dollars if you fail to turn up."

My motivation shifted completely. A second ago I was prepared to contact the garage, now I just rebelled. I didn't feel like calling them at all. The word "MUST" and their threat to charge me 50 dollars, challenged – as in many other situations – a need I really value, namely freedom; the freedom to choose what to do, when to do it and how.

I couldn't help a little embarrassed chuckle and became surprised at how strong my reaction was. As a matter of fact the situation gave me a taste of how important my need for freedom is, and I decided to protect it, in order not to end up rebelling. My way to meet this need, at that moment, was to imagine what needs Per-Eric – who had signed the letter from the garage – wanted to have met. My guess was that he wanted support to serve as many customers as possible. It would have made a big difference to me if he, himself, had expressed his needs and also paid attention to the need for freedom we all have and want respected. He could have written something like this:

Since we have a month long waiting list for customers who want their car serviced, it would make it easier for us if you - as soon as possible – let us know if the appointed time does not suit you. If so we will be able to give the appointed time to someone else and thereby use our mechanics and premises more effectively. That is our way to keep the prices low.

What a pleasure it would have been for me to call Per-Eric had he sent me a letter like this, with a request and not a demand and even a threat. My inner revolt would have turned into delight over the fact that I could contribute to the continued effectiveness of the garage and that someone else might get the car serviced a bit faster.

Key Differentiation 7

"Classical Giraffe" versus "Idiomatic Giraffe"

7

With **Classical Giraffe** we mean to stricly use the four components in NVC: Observation, Feeling, Need and Request. We follow this form precicely both when we express ourselves honestly or listen with empathy to others.

When we speak **Idiomatic Giraffe** we use NVC in a more everyday manner more suited to the situation we are in and the person we are communicating with. "Idiomatic Giraffe" focuses more on creating connection than on exact wording. Regardless of how we speak – classical or idiomatic – we can focus on connecting with empathy and honesty.

Making a empathic guess with "classical Giraffe" might sound like this:

"I wonder if you — when you saw what Mats did today — felt downhearted and disappointed, because your need for care and respect was not met?"

"Idiomatic Giraffe" might in the same situation say something like:

"I guess you have had better days in your life and would have appreciated getting a little more care and respect from Mats?"

When "classical Giraffe" expresses itself with honesty it may sound like this: *"When I see that it is five o'clock and realize that none of the three things I promised the boss to finish today is ready, I feel stressed out and anxious as I need to act with integrity. Would you be willing to write the summary of our report?"*

"Idiomatic Giraffe" might express the same thing this way:

"I really need some help, would you write the summary of our report for me?"

"Classical Giraffe" says:

"I wonder if you are upset because you were not included in the

decision making, since you have a need for community, to be part of a team. Would you like to hear how this came about?"

And the same in "idiomatic Giraffe":
"Guess you are pretty upset because you had wanted to have a part in the decision making?"

7

Reflection

When we focus on teaching or learning the basics of NVC, we often use so called "classical Giraffe". This is to enhance the clarity and get a step closer how we can communicate if we want to create connection. It might sound a bit stiff and strange but is is part of the learning situation.

There are also other occasions when it is helpful to use this more formal way of expressing ourselves with the help of the four components. My partner and I remind each other to change from "idiomatic Giraffe" to "classical Giraffe" when we sense a conflict coming on. Especially if we don't know if our next comment will help support connection or not, when we want to make sure we are clear in our communication. As soon as we are connected we can – if we want to – let go of using the four components, continue focusing on making further connection.

One of us, in this case me - but it could as well have been my partner – may start by saying in frustration: "Yes, but if you could just show some consideration for other people's needs ..."

My partner interrupts:
"I see, all I hear from you right now is criticism. Are you willing to say it again and use observations, feelings, needs and requests?"

My answer – after taking a deep breath and really making sure I want to say 'yes' to his request:

"Okay, I'll try again. When I discover that you have taken the last chocolate bar without asking me if I also wanted some, I feel disappointed, because I would have loved for us to have shared it."

My partner helps me to become even clearer:
"I need to hear what you want from me right now, otherwise it is easy for me to feel guilty, and I don't think that's your intent. What do you want from me right now?"

I think it over and then answer:
"I think what I need most of all right now is for you to understand how frustrating it was for me to see all the chocolate gone, are you willing to tell me what you just heard me say?"

When we trust the intention behind the words we usually connect again.

If people do not trust the intention behind what is said "classical Giraffe" may, sometimes, lead to resistance instead of connection.

If we stick strictly to the four components we may evoke irritation as others might think we are hiding behind a "formula" or that we are trying to sound as if we are superior to others in one way or another. If that is the case it is important that we know how to use "idiomatic Giraffe" and at the same time convey our intention to create a two-way connection.

Key Differentiation 8

"Living Giraffe" versus "Doing Giraffe"

8

With every language we learn – except with our mother tongue – we go through different phases. We study vocabularies and grammar rules and little by little we dare to practice talking and with some training we speak with fluency, use the nuances of the language and find our own wording.

When we **"live Giraffe"** we focus on connection and we alternate between listening with empathy and expressing ourselves with honesty. Sometimes we express ourselves with the help of the four components – observation, feeling, need and requests – sometimes we express ourselves in other ways. When we **"live Giraffe"** we have internalized the basic assumptions underlying NVC in how we relate to others and ourselves.

When we "do Giraffe" we have the intention to connect, but our main focus is on doing it "right". We use the four components - observations, feelings, needs and requests – to express ourselves with honesty or listen empathically. We might have forgotten that the purpose is on creating connection not on talking or listening in a certain way.

When introducing NVC we usually practice the four compo-

nents, words, and grammar, in order to prepare the participants for real life; to dare to try "doing it" and "living it". If we practice NVC, with the intention to connect – we make it a habit to relate to others in this way. Step by step– we contribute to building the confidence that everybody's needs will be considered.

It can be devastating to use the four components of NVC as a tool purely in situations where something has "gone wrong" and without the intention to connect.

8

If, for example, our children do something we dislike and we then, and only then, use NVC, they may start connecting the language itself to unpleasant situations. When they hear expressions like: "When I see ...I feel ...because I need ..." there is an imminent risk that they will think: "Oh, I must have done something wrong again; mother has started using that weird way to express herself again."

Reflection

We do not claim it is easy to "live Giraffe". I want to give an example of my own first fumbling efforts.

One of the assumptions behind NVC is that we want to contribute to one another when we can do so willingly. When I first studied NVC it soon became obvious to me what a gift it is to give one's full presence to someone. I decided to do it as often as I could and I soon found it difficult to say "no" if someone asked me to listen to what they were up against. I started listening in that way even when I did not really want to. I had made the choice to listen emphatically, but forgot the honesty-part of it. I "did Giraffe". It was especially difficult with one of my friends. My inability to say "no" came at a high cost to our relationship.

During one period she could call me several times a week and express distress about things happening in her life. On many of these occasions I listened to her longer than I actually wanted to. A feeling of dislike was growing in me and I didn't want to hear from her at all. Every time she called I noticed I became tense and prepared myself for the worst. I could hear she was in deep pain and in need of support and empathy. Consequently I said "yes" and listened, led by my need for love and a wish to contribute though I didn't feel totally free.

Eventually, I had had enough and said "no" when she called and, I am sad to say, my refusal was not brought forward in the most connecting way. Each time, when I had continued to listen to her pain and had "done Giraffe" when I was not fully willing, it made me really irritated and tired.

After one of those rather upsetting "sessions" it became crystal clear to me that she, in fact, would have appreciated had I told her straight out I was not willing to listen to her any more. It was enormously painful for her, to hear, that I had continued talking and listening to her while I would have preferred to do something else. It took us a long time to repair the broken trust and we both paid a high price because of my reluctance to say "no" in time.

I have heard similar stories from people who have just discovered the beauty and power of empathic listening. As soon as you begin to understand the potential impact of empathy, it may become extra challenging to say "no" when someone expresses pain and wishes to be heard. Instead it is too easy to start using NVC as a tool and to "do Giraffe" rather than to manifest your desire to really be present, with the other, in empathic listening and in honesty.[1]

8

1. Read more about the intention behind NVC in Marshall B. Rosenberg's book Nonviolent Communication, a language for life. PuddleDancer Press.

Key Differentiation 9

"Honesty in Giraffe" versus "Honesty in Jackal"

9

Honesty in Giraffe: With the help of NVC we focus on honestly saying what is going on in us - what is alive in us. We say what we have observed – what we have seen and heard – what we feel, need and wish for or want.

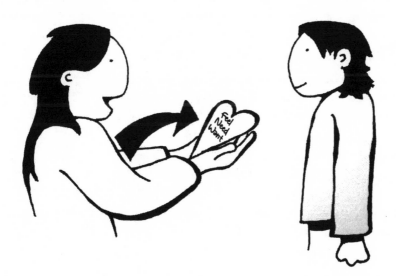

Honesty in Jackal: We express our opinions, what we believe and what we think about others. This kind of honesty has something to do with our cultural imprinting.

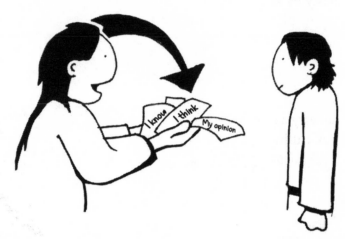

I might think that someone is a "racist" or "an insensitive idiot" and discover that my thinking is a hindrance for a connection with that person.

Someone is describing the atmosphere in our workplace as "crude but hearty". Instead of saying "what an insensitive idiot", either to myself or out loud, using "honesty in Jackal",

I can use "honesty in Giraffe" and say: "When I hear you say the atmosphere is 'crude but hearty', I feel worried because I have witnessed many incidents when people here experienced the crude part but not the hearty one, and I want everyone to feel safe here. Are you willing to tell me what, if anything, you appreciate about the behavior you call 'crude'?"

The person saying something that others may experience as "crude" is often not aware that their comments and words do sometimes evoke pain in others. And the others do not always tell the person, out of fear to be met with more of the same.

Reflection

Many of us have heard others describe their attitude towards honesty by saying something like:

"Yes but I'm frank – I'm always honest with my opinion! If I think someone is a racist – then I'll say so because I value honesty."

9

In this case this key differentiation may serve you. When we express ourselves "honestly in Giraffe" we want to consider our need for honesty as well as our need to care for others.

Instead of calling someone a "racist" I might say:

"This week I have heard you call three other people 'f-ing wogs', which upsets me since I value respect and consideration. I wonder if you are willing to tell me why you call them names?

Remember that if you judge others because you think they communicate in a way that is not showing respect, you are yourself being judgmental.

The purpose of NVC is to create connection and judgments easily interfere with that. You can, if you listen to judgments, your own and others', use them to guide you towards needs that are not being met. When you find the need, you can connect with others, no matter how they express themselves.

Key Differentiation 10

"Screaming in Jackal" versus "Screaming in Giraffe"

10

"We want to be loved,
for want thereof, admired
for want thereof, to be feared
for want thereof, detested and despised.
We want to instill some kind of feeling in others.
Our hearts freeze confronted with emptiness and seek
connection at any price."

HJALMAR SÖDERBERG[1]

Imagine two people crying out the pain in their broken hearts; one is screaming in "Giraffe" and the other in "Jackal". How can you distinguish between them? I guess you have heard many more "Jackal screams" than "Giraffe screams", so probably the most familiar one is the "Jackal scream".

A **"scream in Jackal"** contains accusations, judgments, moralizing, should, musts, rights and wrongs plus other verbal attacks.

When we "scream in Giraffe" we might do it in a loud voice to give weight to our message, but the words used to describe our feelings, needs and requests are used with the intention to connect. This scream comes from someone who wants to stand up for their own needs and the needs of others as well.

A person screaming in "Jackal" might sound like this:
"You are a self-centered idiot thinking of no one but yourself! But just go on! Stick to yourself and don't think about us!"

When someone screams in "Giraffe" it might sound like this:
"I'm so frustrated, because I want to get through to you, and I don't know how. I long for more connection and wonder if you are willing to tell me what is going on in you right now?"

---

1. Söderberg, Hjalmar (2005), Doktor Glas. Albert Bonniers förlag.

No matter how we scream - in "Jackal" or in "Giraffe" - our intention may be to make the other person change their behavior. A person screaming in "Giraffe" wants to do it by making their own and the other person's needs and requests known and clear. Those who scream in "Jackal" want to make others change their behavior by blaming, or by threatening them with some kind of punishment. In our culture this is common.

Sometimes NVC is perceived as a way to relate to life, by showing endless understanding of what is alive in another person. As a matter of fact, the key to connection is the balance between our own needs and the needs of the other. Therefore, it is of importance how I express myself when I'm upset or when I know of no other way than to raise my voice if I want to get through to the other person.

Key Differentiation 11

"No in Jackal" versus "No in Giraffe"

11

A **no in Jackal** is motivated by rules, duties, policies and thoughts about what is right and what is wrong, what is normal and what is appropriate. It does not necessarily reflect what the person saying "no" actually wants. Behind such a "no" there may be a fear of punishment or a wish to be accepted. A "no" in "Jackal" could also be an attempt to punish someone

A no in Giraffe is based on a wish to consider the universal needs of everyone involved. Such a "no" often involves a concept of what he or she is saying "yes" to, when they say "no".

A no in "Giraffe" can also be used to intervene in order to protect life, health, worldly goods or other basic ideas, things we value by refusing to consent to do something that conflicts with those values.

D aniel, are you willing to make ten copies of this CD? I have so many friends who want to buy it from me. Please! I really need some money and you'll get paid.

Daniel knows it is illegal to copy CDs to sell, but regardless of its illegality, the fact is he does not want to do what Patrick is asking of him. Last week he had asked Patrick, who is old enough to buy alcohol, to buy a case of beer for him[1], but Patrick had refused, so Daniel thought he now indeed had the right to say "no".

11

Daniel:

"You said 'no' when I asked you to buy beer for me last week, so why should I do you a favor when you refuse to do me one?"

Patrick was disappointed and accused Daniel of blackmailing him.

Had Daniel known how to say "no in Giraffe" perhaps he would have said something like this:

When I hear that you want me to make me ten copies of this CD so you can sell them to others, I feel irritated. I want more balance in our relationship. I appreciate our friendship and want to contribute to you, but I want to protect my own integrity, so I am saying 'no' to your request. At the same time, I want us to find another way for you to get some extra money, what do you say to that?

In everyday language Daniel could have said: "I do not want to do it, I'm cross with you because of what happened last week, but more important I want to stick to the law. I want us to find another way for you to get some money. OK?"

---

1 This happened in Sweden, where liquor with alcohol content over 3.5% can only be sold in state-regulated liquor stores, and only to those over age 20.

Key Differentiation 12

"Saying I am sorry in Giraffe" versus "Saying I am sorry in Jackal"

12

When we **say we are sorry in Giraffe** we start by trying to understand which of the other person's needs were not met when we acted as we did. We try to find out what they want to request from us now. If and when he or she is prepared to hear our side of 'the story' we tell him or her. We do it by telling what need of ours we tried to meet, when we did what we now wish undone.

When we **say we are sorry in Jackal** we do it by telling the other person what we did wrong. We tell them that we think we are bad, and we are ashamed of our actions. Sometimes we promise 'never to do it again' and add that we are prepared to accept any penalty imposed on us.

Saying I am sorry in Jackal is usually something we have been told to do from a young age, and it is often devoid of meaning. It may have an undertone of 'I am not really sorry but I am only saying so to get it over and done with'.

We have all probably heard ourselves and others say something like:

"I'm sorry, it was terrible of me to do so but I'll never do it again."

12

That is the way we have usually been taught to express ourselves: We did something "wrong" and promise never to do it again.

These promises - not to do it again – are empty words when we repeat them over and over again and ask for forgiveness each time.

"Now I have made a fool of myself again, not just one time but several, I'm absolutely hopeless, yes, that's what I am. I don't deserve your forgiveness, but I'm asking for it anyway".

To ask for forgiveness in this manner and say you accept punishment - saying some prayers or paying some kind of restitution - is institutionalized in our culture and most of us are familiar with it. An alternative way to say you are sorry sounds like this:

"I'm really sorry to discover that my actions have inflicted so much pain on you, and I absolutely want to hear more about how my actions have affected you."

I listen emphatically to the other person, before I say what impact my actions have had on me. When I have heard what my actions meant to the other person, I mourn the choices I made that led me to act as I did. To mourn one's actions is different from being ashamed of them. When I mourn, I listen to what effect my actions have had, what needs were not met by what I said or did and how this insight will influence me. My needs as well as the needs of others are important to me.

Key Differentiation 13

"Empathy Focusing on Content" versus "Empathy Focusing on Process"

13

When we listen with **empathy focusing on content** we listen to what someone tells us about what happened; we pay attention to the words being used and from what is said we guess what feelings were alive in them and what needs were not met when it happened.

When we listen with **empathy focusing on process**, we listen to what is alive in the person, what feelings and needs are alive in him or her right now, at this very moment while we are listening. The same differentiation is valid if we listen to ourselves. We may focus on the story we tell ourselves about what happened, and how we felt then, or feel right now thinking about it and what needs we have at the moment.

Reflection

Barbara called her former colleague Ben. She was in despair and angry at the same time, after a meeting in her workplace where a discussion about a suggested reorganization had taken place.

13

"It was bloody terrible yesterday" she said, *"no one listened when I tried to say something; everyone was just thinking about themselves and what they had to say, about what they wanted; it's hopeless. We didn't even get close to a dialogue. Everything is as it has always been."*

For Ben - who had chosen to leave the company before the reorganization plan was presented – the situation was familiar. Most of all, he was curious to hear what Barbara and his former colleagues had to say about the meeting. At the same time he wanted to contribute and said:

"So, I guess you would have loved to be heard when you said - if people don't listen to one another there will be no dialogue."

They were still talking about Barbara's story and what had happened, when Barbara continued:

"Yes, it's like this every time, we never get anywhere and it feels so hopeless to spend my time in yet another meeting like this."

If Ben had listened with focus on the process when Barbara told him about the meeting, he could have heard what she was feeling at this very moment. He could have asked something like:

"Do you feel sad when you think about the meeting because you long for a situation where everybody is being listened to?"

Barbara may agree:
"Yes, it's like this at every meeting."

And Ben continues listening to what is alive in her.

"So, what you say is you get into despair when you think about what you would love to see change? I guess you want to feel hopeful that you are moving forward to where you can reap what you have sowed."

Key Differentiation 14

"Empathy Focusing on Needs" versus "Empathy Focusing on Unmet Needs"

14

According to one of the basic assumptions of NVC all people have the same universal needs. All our needs are, in different ways, important for our survival and our wellbeing. Our feelings signal to us whether our needs are being met or not. Our needs are neither positive nor negative and we do whatever we can to have them met even if we are not always successful.

When we listen we can listen with **empathy focusing on the need** (here symbolized by a sun). We can, for example say: "My guess is you long for togetherness", if the person talks about a need that is not being met. We "transform" our thoughts about what someone is missing to something we assume they long for to scatter the clouds that hide the needs.

If we listen with **empathy focusing on unmet needs** we guess at the needs and formulate our guess as to what we assume someone is missing. Often the need we express is a guess that is formulated by a negation. For example:

*"I guess you are experiencing **not** being seen?"* if the person has made such an indication. We stay with what they are missing.

Some examples to illustrate the

difference:

*"Are you irritated because you **aren't** experiencing respect?*

Compared to:

"Are you irritated because respect is so valuable to you?"

Or: *"Do you feel disappointed because you **don't** feel free to choose?*

Compared to:

"Do you feel disappointed because you value freedom to choose so highly?"

*"Are you sad because your need for togetherness is **not** being met?"*

Reflection

I asked Karen. My guess might help Karen to find a deeper connection to the sadness she feels because she is missing togetherness. But a guess, where a negation is used - as in my guess written above – will, eventually, cause my support to be experienced more as sympathy than as empathy.[1]

14

If Karen hears my guess as sympathy, she might dig herself deeper into despair and self-pity. When we guess as I did, we are focusing on the cloud hiding the sun instead of on the ever shining sun itself.

When a person is wallowing in self-pity[2] they easily lose their connection to the "sun" although it is always present.[3] We can't see the sun because our umbrella is hiding it.

If my guessing had focused on the need, I could have asked Karen:
"Are you sad because commmunity is something you really value?"

When we listen with empathy, we want to encourage people to listen to their feelings and connect them to their needs.

1. See Key Differentiation 17
2. See Key Differentiation 21.
3. See Key Differentiation 2.

In our guessing we link their feeling directly to a need that might lay behind the feeling. By doing so, we help them find "the sun" more effectively and evoke their longing to take further steps in order to have their need met When it, for example, becomes obvious for a person that they long for community, it is easier for them to take measures to get that need met.[4]

4. Rosenberg, Marshall (2012) Nonviolent Communication, a language of life. PuddleDancer Press.

Key Differentiation 15

"Stating" versus "Guessing"

15

Whether we express ourselves by stating or by guessing depends on how we view what is alive in others.

When we **state** something about someone we make our assumptions based on our observations and our thoughts around what we think is alive in the other person. Sometimes we ask the other person to confirm that what we have stated corresponds with what is going on in them.

When we **guess** what is alive in someone, we do it to strengthen our ability to be present in the moment with that person. We recognize our guesses may not be what the other is experiencing.

Ultimately our intention influences whether we approach others by guessing or stating.

When we - in our own opinion – think we know what is alive in the other, our intention can easily be to have our own thoughts confirmed rather than to connect with the other.

- When we choose to connect by guessing, we let go of all static statements and are fully open for whatever happens every moment.

- When we guess, our intention is to be with the other in their process. We express our guesses out loud, if we are losing our connection with the other, or, if we think they need our support to get on in their process.

Reflection

I remember a situation when my father-in-law was talking about the works of art and artists and I had an increasing problem with keeping interested.

15

My thoughts were focused on *why* he was talking about this. Several times I was a hair's breadth away from interrupting him to say something like:

"I know that you like fine arts, but I'm actually not very interested in this."

Instead I decided to try to find out why the subject was so important to him. As he talked about the works of art and artists I guessed creativity was involved in one way or another. I made a brief guess in his next short pause and instead of telling what was alive in me, I asked:

"So, you like art because you value creativity?"

He stopped for a moment. When he answered his speech was slower than before:

"No, it's not that … it is more about … I do really see God in their work."

I was silent for a while and then slowly asked:

"And do you find meaning in your life when you are connected to that?"

He nodded and was silent. We connected without me interrupting or asking him to say more. I understood and recognized his need for meaning and spirituality, as they are important needs for me too. As soon as we touched on universal human needs it became easier for me to really enjoy his detailed talk about the works of art and artists.

Key Differentiation 16

"Guessing Intellectually" versus "Guessing Empathically"

16

We can´t discover new oceans until we have the courage to lose sight of land.

ANONYMOUS

Guessing intellectually, we want to understand and make guesses - sometimes based on our own experiences. We guess what is alive in someone else and try to find solutions or provide explanations we think can help the person to handle his or her own feelings.

When we are **guessing empathically,** we try to understand what is alive in another person. We do so, trusting that our presence and the connection we establish will support the other in connecting with their feelings and needs. If we are uncertain or lose the connection, we might guess at the person's needs, thereby perhaps helping him or her in connecting to unconscious needs.

The difference between trying to understand someone intellectually and to understand through empathy lies in where we have our focus. When we guess intellectually, we want to find solutions and often we dwell on what has happened. When we listen empathically we try to stay in the present with what is alive

in the other person. We do not try to find explanations or to come up with solutions; our focus is entirely on connecting. Sometimes, the difference between guessing intellectually and guessing empathically is subtle. The person who wants to be heard might, regardless of how we listen, connect to their feelings and needs on their own.1

16

Reflection

My son was used to me trying to listen empathically. One unusually hectic morning he spilled his milk all over the floor. He - at this occasion not yet three years old - saw my frustration and asked:

"Are you disappointed, mommy?"

The mere fact that he asked the way he did was heartwarming and in the midst of my frustration I chuckled and immediately he asked:

"Are you happy now?"

He could easily change his guesses as he followed what was alive in me without making static analyses of my feelings[1].

Sometimes the opening message in a dialog is just the tip of an iceberg. Most of the iceberg is under the surface. This is also true of our feelings; they are often stronger on the inside than what is shown on the outside. If we halt and do not jump to conclusions at the

1. You can read more in Nonviolent Communication, a language of life, by Marshall Rosenberg. Puddle Dancer Press. Chapters 7-9.

first words a person says, but listen with empathy, we will often hear deeper feelings expressed than those at first mentioned.

Initially, people often show just a small part of what is alive in them, but when we have shown that we really want to listen they may feel safe and invite us to share more of their reality.

When people experience that they are being listened to, they may connect on a deeper level with what is alive in them and more and more of their inner "iceberg" becomes visible to themselves and to the person listening.

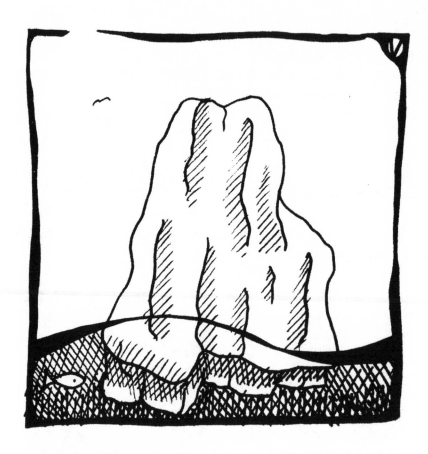

Key Differentiation 17

"Sympathy" versus "Empathy"

17

When we listen with **sympathy** we listen to what the person has to say and we reflect back by telling how the story made us feel, how we understand what the person is going through and feels, based on our own experiences.

When we listen with **empathy** we try to hear what the other person feels and needs; i.e. what is alive in them. If we think we can contribute to a connection or if we lose track we may come up with a guess.

Empathy can be silent, but we can also mirror back to the other person what we have heard to confirm our presence. The difference between empathy and sympathy can be illustrated with a picture from a mountain crest. I stand on one of the peaks. On a nearby peak stands another person.

When I listen with sympathy, I listen to what he or she can see from that peak and then I tell them what I observe from mine.

If I use empathy I slide down from my mountain to join the other person, and try to see what he or she is observing from that peak.

When we listen with empathy, our focus is on what is going on in the other person; what is alive in them. When we listen with sympathy, we connect to our own feelings in relation to what the

other person is experiencing. If we are sympathetic we agree, feel sorry for or perhaps even put the blame on a third person, saying that he or she caused the feelings in the person we are listening to. We might also start telling similar stories from our own experiences, to show our understanding. Sadly enough, this seldom gives us the quality of connection we long for.

If a person is listened to with sympathy he or she might eventually feel understood, but we also run the risk that it will make matters worse. Sympathy might strengthen the idea that the feelings are caused by what someone else said or did, which might contribute to the creation of enemy images. If a person thinks that the actions of someone else caused their feelings, the person may find it difficult to recognize his or her own needs. In this case, a feeling of powerlessness may emerge and thoughts of revenge may appear.

Sympathy between members of a group may contribute to a thinking based on "we and them". This may strengthen the solidarity between the members, but possibly at the cost of relations with people outside the group.

During one period I was working with a large organization which had problems with its service towards their customers. The employees expressed that they had the support they needed within their team. I joined them for some time and observed a variety of sympathetic behavior. When one employee told a colleague about a problem experienced with a customer he or she was often backed-up, pepped up or pitied. Of course they supported each other, but it was done in a way which often broadened the distance to a certain customer or to customers in general.

17

For me it is important that we connect and to pay attention to everybody's needs – and with sympathy we easily forget to consider all needs and every person as equally important. During my time with this organization everyone were taught to listen with empathy. Although we did not talk about the relations to their customers, the attitude towards them was changed radically. Each could listen to the other in a way that increased creativity without diminishing the supportive team spirit. It also became easier to hear what the customers needed, which led to service improvements.

A year later, I was working with employees in another organization and thought I could use the same concept again. Although we practiced how to listen empathically, not very much changed. The complaints from their customers continued unreduced, and customer relations were regarded as difficult as ever. When we talked about it, it became obvious that employees were so used to getting sympathy that they continued to hear my empathy guesses as "I agree with you".

It was not until we practiced the "dance" of both honesty and empathy that a shift was experienced. I learned that empathy, without honesty, too easily can be perceived as an assent or as sympathy, especially if that is the expectation.

Sympathy – in the sense of feeling sorry for or to comfort – might in some situations be very supporting and even life promoting.

When my five-year old is hurt it seems, at least to start with, that he is neither interested in empathy nor in sympathy. All he wants me to do is to look at the wound, to see how long, deep or bloody it is. He also wants me to listen as he tells exactly where and how it happened, for example what he stumbled over.

One thing we can do for people who have gone through life-threatening crises, accidents, fires, or other traumatic experiences is to help them to recall what really happened. Not to dwell on it but to establish what really happened. When that is done we can continue and listen for feelings, needs and other reactions. Perhaps this is what my son is trying to obtain even if his crisis is a minor one, at least in my view.

Key Differentiation 18

"Advice" versus "Empathy"

18

When we give **advice** we suggest how we think someone may proceed, to be able to solve a problem or find a new way to handle something they feel badly about, or even find overwhelming. Advice – "or good advice" as it is often called – is based on the "advicers" own experiences, real or fictitious. The intention is to contribute, often in the firm conviction that what they say will be a support for the other person.

When we listen with **empathy** we listen to what the other person says about his or her situation. We try to support them and – if we think it will contribute – we guess what they need and long for in the situation they describe. If we listen with empathy and the other person– with or without our verbal support – connects to needs they might have disregarded, the chances are good that they will themselves come up with strategies to meet those needs. If they don't, they might ask for advice, and we have the choice to give it or not.

In contrast to empathy, advice seldom helps the person to connect to their deeper needs. What we often overlook when we give advice, is that the person receiving it often has a deeper insight than others into their own situation and therefore advice may not bring in something new.

Advice may be valuable if you get stuck and don't know how to handle situations perceived as obstacles. And even if someone starts a conversation asking for advice it may still contribute more to connection to guess the needs behind their request for advice.

If someone asks for advice – after having been listened to with empathy – they will probably find it more supportive than if they get advice without having asked for it or if they have asked for guidance "out of habit".

Reflection

Emma's live-in partner Oskar has met another women and he has decided to move in with his new love and start a family. Emma is sad and frustrated when she tells her mother about it. Her mother tries to contribute by giving advice Emma hasn't asked for:

18

"Yes but you must understand that the best thing you can do now is to let go of Oskar and go on with your life. Don't stay at home and dwell on this, but start dating other men, there are so many nice young men out there!"

Advice like this might make Emma ashamed of her choices. Or she might feel angry and lonely while thinking that no one understands her.

The advice from her mother – for sure well intended – might start a downward spiral where Emma tries to protect herself and says:

"That's easy for you to say. Especially since you have never been abandoned; you were the one who left father!"

The mother takes Emma's answer as a means of guilt-tripping her, and she doesn't hear that behind Emma's words there is an even stronger need for empathy. Rage is growing in the mother and she tells herself that Emma is ungrateful and ought to understand that her mother is trying to support her:

"No, I certainly haven't, but it's obvious that your situation will not change for the better if you continue to be embittered and ungrateful, and if you shut yourself off from the outside world."

To give advice is an attempt to contribute, but if the person receiving it doesn't want it, the risk is obvious that it – as in this example – creates distance instead of connection and is of no true help for any of the people involved. The situation began with *one* frustrated person and ends up with *two*.

If Emma's mother had listened with empathy from the start their dialogue might have developed as follows:

"I'm heartbroken and actually I don't know what to do. I have no desire to do anything at all. I haven't left the apartment for weeks except when I went shopping for some food and cat litter."

"I can hear that you feel bad about it and want me to hear how tough this is for you right now."

"Yes, (sobbing) *it's absolutely unbearable that Oskar has left and that they have already decided to get married and have children."*

(Short pause)

"I guess that what's happening is scary and painful because you really valued your relationship so much?"

"Yes I miss him so much ... (crying)*... I'm aching all over."*

"I can hear that he means very, very much to you and it sounds as if you long for love, to give and to receive. And that you are mourning right through your body because this is so important to you."

"Yes I long for love, but I don't want love from someone who doesn't want to stay by me."

"You want to be loved and to trust that love. Is that so?"

"Yes, I want it to be for real!"

A couple of similar exchanges later when Emma's mother has listened with empathy:

"You know Emma, now when you have told me what is going on in you, I wonder if you are willing to hear what has come alive in me?"

"Yes, I will. It feels really good that we can talk like this. That makes me feel safe in the midst of all the turbulence."

When both parties tell what is alive in them and listen empathically they might reach a point where Emma asks her mother for advice. She perhaps concludes that advice and others' experience is what best can meet her needs right now.

And the chances are good that a situation that began with *one* frustrated person will end up with *two* who feel confident that they will continue to support one another.[1]

18

---

1. Read more on Empathy, in Nonviolent Communication, a language of life, by Marshall Rosenberg. Puddle Dancer Press. Chapters 7-9.

Key Differentiation 19

"Listen With Empathy" versus "Consoling"

19

When we **listen with empathy** as well as when we are consoling, our intention is to be present with the other. The difference lies both in *how* we listen, *what* we listen for and how we *act* in relation to their feelings.

When we listen with empathy, we listen for feelings and needs and try to follow what is alive in the other person moment by moment. Empathy can be wordless, but sometimes words are used to reflect back what we have heard the other person say. We can ask questions if we lose track, or guess if we think that will help the other person to connect inwards.

When we **console** we listen to what the other is telling us about something they are sad about – or what we think they are sad about. We try to contribute by suggesting different strategies to "get rid of" the sadness or encourage them to find ways to handle the situation.

Consoling and comforting can be done in various ways. Besides using different distractions or bodily contact like hugs we might say something like:

"I'm sure it will go away" or *"I know you'll manage, you are so strong!"*

Reflection

I remember the heartache, the almost insurmountable deep-felt grief I felt as a teen ager. My pain was literally beyond words; I could not talk about it. But many people noticed and above all there were people consoling:

"You are such a cute and charming girl, I'm sure you'll soon find a new love", or *"oh yes, don't worry, we have all experienced that, you'll overcome."*

19

When I look back now, I can't remember one single person who listened with empathy to me. I guess it would have made a big difference for me had someone just said:

"I imagine you are longing for someone to just sit down and listen to you right now?"

Instead the school doctor prescribed some pills and his nurse comforted me and my best friend put her arms around my shoulders and promised me the pain would pass as soon as I found a new boyfriend. The guy, with whom I did the laboratory lessons in physics, comforted me in his own way by writing me a note saying that he wanted to be the apple I ate, that at least made me smile. At home the message was more or less, even if it was not said out loud *"pull yourself together and make sure you pass your exam!"*

The needs I was longing to meet were respect and to mourn. I wanted others to see me, my anguish and to be listened to with empathy, but at that time I was not aware of what I was longing for. Now, many years later I try to use my own experience and practice the power of empathic listening to connect to people I come across on my own life journey.

A young relative told me:

"I'm really so sad and have no idea what to do. You know my girl-friend wants to break up ... What do you suggest?

Even if it is worded as if they want some "good advice" I refrain from giving it to start with. I try first to listen and pay attention to needs that want to come out into the open. After these are clear i give the advice I might have.

Key Differentiation 20

"Mourning" versus "Giving up"

We use the word **mourning** when we are focused on what we feel right now, in regard to something that happened a little while or a long time ago, that we are unhappy about. It may be something we did or did not do that was not in harmony with our or someone else's needs. On our own or with the support of others we try to connect with the need or needs behind our distress.

We can ask someone to listen empathically to find the unmet needs and perhaps also work out strategies to have those needs met now. When we mourn we don't feel shame or guilt, blame ourselves or become depressed, something that easily happens if we think that we did something wrong.

When we **give up**, we try to "put the lid on" and forget or ignore what happened that we might have needed to grieve.

When we give up we have usually lost connection to our own needs. We then easily end up in passivity because we can't find the strategies that could have helped us feel better. We run the risk of getting stuck in ideas about "right and wrong" and what we or others ought to have done differently.

The big difference between mourning and giving up is where we put our focus when we have experienced something that awakens our feelings of distress. A person giving up tries in different ways to escape from needs that are not met. Perhaps they don't manage to look for them, they want peace and quiet or don't have the "tools" – or perhaps they are denying that they have needs or that there are tools to handle them.

A person mourning is instead focused on their needs and thereby has a better chance to find strategies to have them met.

Mourning is a process where the connection to needs is essential and the mourning is per se a universal need. When we give up, we shut ourselves off from our inner driving force and might find it difficult to proceed with our lives.

Reflection

20

I think about a married couple I knew, who many, many years ago decided to follow separate courses. In addition to preconceived ideas from those around them, economic problems and changed standard of living, the way they handled their grief had an effect on their lives.

For her, a new love moved in and life was - at least on the surface - good for her and she didn't mourn. For him, the grief was almost paralyzing and after some time he asked for help and connected to his need for the community that was not met. He mourned the separation and the loss of everyday contact with his two daughters, the cats and the beautiful surroundings where they had previously lived. And he mourned the dreams he had not fulfilled. Nothing had turned out the way he had wanted.

Five years later the picture had changed. He had found a way to connect to his daughters and he had found a house where he was happy. The neighbor's cat sometimes dropped by purring with content, rubbing against his legs. He had lots of friends who loved to visit him and the girls. And he loved his job!

For his ex-wife the situation was different. She was on and off sick leave for a couple of years, and the man she met right after the divorce left her a year later. Since then she has lived in different relationships. She says herself that she is bitter and finds it difficult to reach out for the helping hands that are there for her. She claims that she was born under an unlucky star and that's the reason for her misery, which explains, according to her, why she always gets into troublesome relationships.

The lives of those two people serve as a reminder that we, even in difficult phases in life, can be empowered and connect to our dreams and driving forces, and thereby find a way to carry on with our lives. I'm also reminded of how distressed I feel when I think of how lack of connection with – or flight from – our own needs can turn our lives into a long painful journey, a journey that can be made even more difficult by society's views about men, women and divorce.

Key Differentiation 21

"Self-empathy" versus "Dwelling on Feelings"

21

Self-empathy:
In situation when we need empathy, and do not find anyone that can listen to us in an empathetic way we can listen to ourselves with empathy. Perhaps we are happy and want to embrace the whole world or we are sad and everything is black as night. We might start with an observation, guess feelings and needs and try to figure out what we might ask of ourselves or someone else

to meet the needs we are connected to.

By **dwelling on feelings** we refer to what happens when we focus on our feelings, without trying to understand what they are actually signaling to us. When we dwell on our feelings we easily get stuck and end up feeling sorry for ourselves, and thereby intensify our thoughts that the situation we are in is impossible to resolve.

Reflection

Does it sometimes happen to you too, that you catch yourself saying something like:

"Why didn't I do this or that, I really wanted to do it but now it's too late?"

If you were longing to do something, that you didn't do after all, you need to mourn it, perhaps for a minute, a day or for years to come. You need to mourn to balance what you were longing for

96

and your reasons for making another choice.

Often our intention to find that balance comes to a halt and we end up "dwelling on feelings", judging, blaming or feeling sorry for ourselves, or blaming others - saying they caused our pain. We easily get stuck in thoughts that we have no power, which might lead us into a spiral of judgmental thoughts towards ourselves and others. We think that we are the victims of circumstances and thereby don't connect to the needs that could have motivated us to act for a change.

21

If instead we choose to listen to our feelings and our needs, when we are accusing ourselves of something we "missed"- for example a journey we never made – we give ourselves a chance to grow from the experience. We can figure out what we can do now or later to have that need met. Perhaps we could go on a trip. Or we might invite friends for a dinner party if our need was excitement and connection. With this kind of self-empathy we might also want to connect to the needs we actually met when we didn't do what we are now regretting. The connection with the needs may give us the strength to act to meet them now, or in the future and under different circumstances.

Key Differentiation 22

"Self -empathy" versus "Acting out Your Feelings"

22

W hen we talk about **self-empathy** in NVC, we refer to a process where we listen to ourselves in the same way as we listen to others with empathy. We listen to what is going on inside us and – regardless of what is happening within – we search for the observations, feelings and needs that have led us to think and act as we do. With the help of self-empathy we try to find strategies that will give us a chance to have our needs met. We debate with ourselves about what we want to ask someone else or what we will ask ourselves. Self-empathy is practiced in the same way whether we are mourning or celebrating.

When we **act out our feelings** they are often manifested physically. We may cry and scream, give a kick or tear our hair, or roar with laughter and jump for joy. We might also, over and over again, talk about our feelings and what we think caused them. To act out one's feelings might be the starting point for self-empathy. But if we stop there and think it is over and done with because we were acting out our feelings, we won't connect to the needs behind those feelings.

If we don't connect to the needs, it becomes difficult to find strategies that could help us meet unmet needs, or help us to see what we could do in order to experience pleasurable feelings more often. Supported by the principles of NVC we listen to ourselves with empathy and connect our feelings to our needs. The feelings will not be experienced as threatening, complicated, or meaningless; instead they rather help us understand what we do need.

When we feel tired and uninspired we can listen to our body to find out if we have a need to rest or perhaps a need of stimulation. If we feel disappointed, our need might be connection and if we feel irritated there is perhaps a need for respect and acceptance.

In our culture we often put the blame for our strong feelings on something others did or said, but there are also those claiming that our strong feelings say more about us than about what someone else did or said. For me it is more inspiring, and gives me more hope, to go a step further than to just handle my reactions on my own or to blame others. I take that step when I link my feelings to my needs and tell others what they said or did that triggered my feelings. When I tell that, I make it clear that the cause of my feelings is my needs. Other people may say or do something, which is the external stimulus, which affected me and was the trigger for those feelings signaling to me that I had an unmet need. If I don't tell the person who triggered my feelings that this is the way I see it, it is more likely that they will find it difficult to eventually change their behavior in order to contribute to me.[1]

---

1. Read more about self-empathy in Rosenberg, Marshall (2003), Nonviolent Communication: A Language of Life. PuddleDancer Press. Chapters 9 and 12.

Key Differentiation 23

"Systems Based on Domination" versus "Systems Based on Needs"

23

In **systems based on domination** we imagine that there is a "right" and a "wrong" way to relate to ourselves, others and the world we live in. We accept the prevailing hierarchical structure where the authorities are given the privilege to exercise power. We also think that certain behaviors are normal and others are not. Furthermore we use labels when describing one another and obey the authorities, often out of fear. By pleading to the authorities as an excuse for our behavior, we disclaim responsibility for our own actions.

The driving force in a system based on domination is rewards and punishments integrated into the system, all the way from ordinary people to the judicial system. People in this kind of system are also often motivated by guilt, shame, duty, 'have to' and obligations.

In systems based on needs we try to consider, and as often as possible meet, needs. We strive to connect internally with ourselves and externally with others, in order to contribute to needs being met. The driving force is our wish to contribute to the well-being of others and the planet. Therefore we give, when we can do so willingly, and receive when the other is giving of free will. We respect authorities and value their contributions.[1]

One difference between the two systems becomes obvious when we observe what happens if someone chooses not to adjust to the system. In systems based on domination - whether they are states or organizations – there is usually some kind of sanctions built into the system. If you violate the law or other rules and regula-

1. See also Key Differentiation 25.

101

tions, implemented by the authorities, you might miss rewards and be punished accordingly - in extreme cases even be tortured or sentenced to death. Also at the individual or group level - within ourselves and in families and small groups - punishments and rewards are used.

In systems based on needs, rules and regulations are the result of mutually reached agreements. A person breaking the agreement can be prevented from doing so if their action could lead to a potentially dangerous situation for the person, for others, or for the environment. When, in a system based on needs, force is used, it is done to protect, never to punish.

23

Reflection

Looking through a newspaper, I read about two youths, 17 and 18 years old, who had been convicted of assault and battery against two rehabilitation therapy assistants while in a juvenile prison. The beating of the therapy assistants, we are informed, started when one of the young men was ordered to put down the hood of his sweatshirt and uncover his head while eating his supper.

When the youngster - despite several reprimands - refused, the two assistants decided to take him to his room. They went up behind him, one on each side and grabbed his arms. When he tried to escape, all three men ended up on the floor. An 18-year-old inmate came to his friend's rescue. The situation became unmanageable and the assistants called the police for support. When the police arrived the 18-year-old had already voluntarily left for the isolation room to cool down.

According to the newspaper article, the 18-year-old told the court that he became outraged and didn't know what to do, when he saw his friend lying on the floor, overpowered by the two assistants.

During the court proceedings the 17-year-old said that his refusal to put down the hood, had to do with the fact, that he, that very day, had had a haircut and was extremely dissatisfied with the way it turned out. He was ashamed and wanted absolutely no one to see his new haircut.

The 17-year-old was sentenced for violently resisting and violence towards a person in authority. The 18-year-old was sentenced for violence towards a person in authority and for petty drug offense. They were both sentenced to continue their stay in the juvenile prison and fined a considerable sum.

Heavy-heartedly I folded the newspaper, pondering over how those involved would have acted, had they lived in a system based on needs rather than on domination.

I guess that people - who are daily at risk in their workplace of ending up in violent situations - feel stressed and insecure, and want to be reassured that they can be protected. Presumably they have learned – as they live in a domination system – that it is very important to "set up clear limits" and that that is the only way to make those youngsters adjust to the rules in force.

In a system based on needs I can hardly imagine a situation like this coming up at all. The young man with the "failed haircut" would have had his need for integrity met and the assistant would have probably easily found other ways to take care of his need for safety and respect, in a more effective way. And I guess that no one would have come up with the idea of forcing a 17-year-old to show himself publicly when he didn't want to.

Key Differentiation 24

"Power With" versus "Power over"

24

Power can be seen as the ability to access emotional and material resources in order to meet needs.

Power with: everybody's needs are important. We use our power, i.e. mobilize our resources, our strengths and our ability to promote, decide on and implement objectives. These can be individual or common objectives that we and others have agreed upon together.

Power over: We act as if it is more important for us to meet our own needs than to meet the needs of others. We may, for example, threaten with punishments or promise rewards, and by so doing, we use our strength and our ability to make others do or say what we want them to. We do it in ways that – at least in the interim – meet some of our needs, disregarding the needs of others.

There is also a concept called *power under.* It deals with the powerlessness people experience, especially in relation to traumatic events such as war, domestic abuse, threats of violence or other events that are, or can be perceived as, life-threatening. Powerlessness can turn oppressed people into oppressors, as they internalize the behavior they have themselves been subjected to. If we understand this side of power we perhaps can find new tools for breaking cycles of violence.[1]

Reflection

I once participated in a team at work, where we found that our performance had come to a complete standstill. Our boss was – understandably – more and more dissatisfied with our results, and the atmosphere in the team was becoming really tense.

No one thought it was at all pleasant when the boss came for his weekly visit to our local office.

When we analyzed the situation within the team, we found that the boss himself was standing in the way of the changes he wanted to see, of course without being aware of this.

But then the boss attended a workshop! And the next weekly team meeting was quite different from the usual. The boss opened the meeting by saying:

"I have just decided that from now on, I want all of you to participate and to have a say in the decision making process.

---

1. Wineman, Steven (2003) Power-Under, Trauma and Nonviolent Social Change.

We looked at each other in surprise and suspicion. I could hardly refrain from starting to teach him what to do differently. After some self-empathy I tried to tell him about my worries. I wondered about our future cooperation if he was to continue to make decisions above our heads, even if he – as in this case – had declared that he wanted to include us in the decision-making process. He said he was welcoming suggestions from us, about what **24** to do differently. After some discussion in the team, we concluded that one thing that would really have made us feel included, was if he had said something like:

"In retrospect I realize that when I opened this meeting by saying 'I have just decided that from now on, I want all of you to participate and to have a say in the decision making process' I probably didn't sound as open and inviting as I wanted to. I wish I had said something in the following direction instead:

I have realized that I haven't let you take part in the decision-making process, and that due to that our work has been less effective than it could have been. I have reflected a lot on this and from now on I would like you to be involved in the decisions on some important questions ahead of us. What do you say about this? Would you like to be part of this? And if so, in what way?"

This may serve as an example of the difference between power over and power with. In this case the team members set up objectives for the boss to consider, and continued to do so until they found ways to cooperate that led them to the desired results.

Key Differentiation 25

"Fear of Authorities" versus "Respect for Authorities"

25

It is often more difficult to listen empathically to people who seem to have more power, status or resources than we ourselves have.
MARSHALL ROSENBERG[1]

The difference between fear of and respect for authorities is apparent from how we react in relation to persons we have labeled "authorities".

Fear of authorities: When we say or do what an "authority" asks us to out of fear of being punished or not being rewarded, we act out of fear of authorities. We act as obedient "subjects" and we don't try to affect the authority's strategy although we may see alternative ways to act. When we fear authorities we often forget to see the human being behind the label, because we are so busy safeguarding ourselves.

Respect for authorities: When we respect someone, labeled as an authority, we pay extra attention to how knowledgeable that person is in his field where he or she is regarded as an "authority". This does not mean that we "blindly" obey or believe in what the person says. On the contrary, we weigh their words and consider in what ways they will serve us. Even if the person is an authority in his or her subject field, we see them primarily as human beings, with feelings and needs exactly like the rest of us.

---

1. Rosenberg, Marshall (2003), Nonviolent Communication: A Language of Life. PuddleDancer Press.

Reflection

We want to draw your attention to the fact that the words authority and authoritarian are often mixed up. A person can be very knowledgeable and skilled – and be labeled authority – within one or several fields, without being authoritarian. The label "authority" could be translated into an observation like: He was familiar with the internal combustion engine design in all ten inspected car models. An observation, when we have judged someone as "authoritarian" could be as below.

"I saw him raise his hand. At the same time he told Charles: "Do as you are told and stop asking silly questions!"

To respect someone's authority, means that we value the knowledge and skills they have within a certain field. When we do so, we often feel calm, safe and grateful. It does not necessarily mean that we will act in accordance with what an "authority" suggests, as respect in this case also includes the respect of our own free will. When we respect an authority, we still see that we have a free choice, which is not something we experience when we fear an authority.

There is a big difference between respecting teachers, bosses doctors or parents only because of their title or label and to respect them because of their knowledge. We can still see them as fellow humans, and as human beings who know more than we do in a certain field. If we look upon them as "bosses" or "teachers" it is easy to lose connection to their needs. A woman we label as a "composer" and who is greatly appreciated by many as an authority when it comes to music – has the same needs for care, respect and acceptance as everyone else. Her ability to create music that might meet needs, tells us nothing about her ability to take care of children or fix a broken engine. If she is in the midst of an unhappy love affair she has the same need for understanding as the rest of us. The mere fact that she is not feeling happy does not have to affect our experience of and appreciation for her music.

25

Key Differentiation 26

"Obeying" versus "Self-Discipline"

26

The difference between obeying and self-discipline lies primarily in *why* we act as we do; what our driving force is.

When we **obey** we act as we do because we tell ourselves that it is our duty, or we tell ourselves that we must do it. Sometimes we act to get - or give ourselves – a reward or to avoid punishment.

When we practice **self-discipline** we act as we do because we choose to, motivated by a wish to meet needs. We see how our actions will serve ourselves and others.

The actual action I take may be exactly the same regardless of why I do it; if I do it to obey or because I have asked myself which needs will be met by my actions. The difference is the joy and energy I feel and how "persistent" I am in carrying out my actions. If I act out of obedience I may stop what I am doing as soon as no one is watching me. Or I do whatever I have been asked to do, but act in such a way, that others will have to pay for it later. It is not unusual that a person motivated by obedience reaches a stage where it might seem as if rebellion or submission, are the only alternatives available.

Reflection

When I hear my inner voice repeatedly tell me what I ought or must do, for example.
"I have to get up earlier in the morning, I must exercise more, I ought to call my mother, I must write an article ..."

26

I can take a deep breath. I know by now, that when I hear demands - you ought to, you must - from my inner voice or from someone else, one part of me starts thinking:
Now I have no choice, I have to do this.

The next moment I start rebelling and tell myself:
I'm indeed free to stay in bed as long as I want to, and I can skip the exercise, forget to call my mother and ignore the article.

If I then take a deep breath, I can reconnect with the needs I wanted to meet in setting up these different goals for how I want to live my life:
I want to run my usual distance in less than an hour before midsummer, call my mother every day to connect on a deeper level, and write an article for the local newspaper before the end of the month.

I recall that I want to take care of my health. In addition I also want to uphold the connection I have with my "running mate" and the unbelievably nice moments we spend together in the sauna after having run till we are all sweaty

And undoubtedly the conversations with my mother meet needs of both community and connection, but how about the article? I still have a struggle with that and I certainly don't enjoy thinking about it. When I discover that thinking about the article is no fun, I realize that I want to reconsider my plan concerning the article, set up new goals and look at what motivates me. For whom am I writing? Am I writing because I find it stimulating or am I writing because I want to be seen, to be a good girl? Do I believe that I have to be a good girl and perform in order to be liked?

Every time I act because I want an external reward and forget the needs behind it, I'm at risk of losing joy in my actions. A call from a friend, who asked me about a detail in my article, made me realize how important the message in the article was, and how much clarity it could bring for so many people; my energy around the article shifted completely. Suddenly I could not get started fast enough. After a round in the forest, a sauna with my friend, and a call to my mother I'm now sitting here writing my article. From the outside looking in, it might seem as if I'm a slave to my goals. But I can assure you it is about just doing it as if it is both play and meaningful.

Key Differentiation 27

"Protective use of force" versus "Punitive use of force"

27

One way to differentiate between protective and punitive use of force is to examine what the person using force is thinking.

MARSHALL ROSENBERG.[1]

When we observe someone acting in a way we comprehend as potentially dangerous, we may try to prevent the person from acting using one of two different approaches.

We can step in with the intention to prevent the person from injuring themselves or others. In that case our approach is **protective use of force**, as we are totally convinced that the person has no intention, what so ever, to cause any harm.

If we, on the other hand, think human beings are basically evil and egoistic creatures, a situation when we think someone is going to do something potentially dangerous makes us intervene. But now, our intention is to teach the person a lesson and in one way or the other punish him or her. In this case our approach is **punitive use of force**. We try to show them what is right and what is wrong – according to us – and we try to make them act as we want them to.

1.Rosenberg, Marshall (2007), (2003), Life-Enriching Education: Nonviolent Communication Helps Schools Improve Performance, Reduce Conflict and Enhance Relationships. PuddleDancer Press.

Many parents may find the following situation familiar.

"Please stop playing computer games!"

Ten minutes later in a slightly louder voice:
"Switch off the computer!"

Another ten minutes later, now with a significantly louder and sharper voice:
"Switch off now, at once! OR
."

This frequently happened to some of my friends. They had an agreement – or perhaps it was just something the parents had unanimously decided – that their children were allowed to play computer games for no more than one hour each weekday evening. When it was time to switch the computer off it was always the same old story, a hullabaloo:

Loud voices, sourpusses, threats of "never more" and threats of "leaving home" and labels like "the silliest mother or father in the universe" or "ungrateful brats". The allegations came thick and fast.

My friends, who had studied NVC, were enormously frustrated by those fights and about not being able to connect with their children. When the situation reoccurred one day after we had discussed the matter in depth, the father realized that he had ignored his own needs for too long.

When he discovered that he once again was on the verge of getting so angry that he just wanted to punish his teenager, he decided to hold on to his needs, instead of coming up with allegations. When his teenager didn't react after having been told three times to switch off the computer, my friend simply switched off the main power switch and all electricity in the house was cut off.

This of course caused an angry outcry. But as my friend was neither irritated nor angry and acted only with the intention to protect his integrity, he was able to listen to and take in his teenager's outrage.

This was the beginning of a dialogue and a cooperation that was far more stable than it would have been had the father not held on to his own needs.

27

Without a follow-up dialogue, my friend's action could have had the opposite effect. When we use our power to protect in a forceful way, it is important that we begin talking as soon as possible in order to continue to focus on connection.

In one of my workshops we were discussing protective use of force. A mother in the group recalled a situation where she had – when her daughter was only four – done exactly that; used her power to protect her daughter. She had rescued her from a herd of angry rams, by flinging her over the wire fence. The daughter was saved and unscathed apart from some scratches on her knees. At least that's what the Mother had thought at the time and since then. Unfortunately they had not talked about what had happened in the immediate aftermath of the incident nor afterwards. Up until womanhood the daughter had viewed the situation in a different way. For over 20 years she had been convinced that her mother had flung her over the fence out of ill will. As the daughter was also participating in my workshop, her lack of trust could at last be repaired.

Key Differentiation 28

"Moralistic Judgments" versus "Value Judgments"

28

Interpretations, criticisms, diagnosis and judgments of others are actually alienated expressions of our unmet needs.

MARSHALL ROSENBERG.[1]

This key differentiation helps us pay attention to when we judge others in terms of right and wrong; "Now you are right or now you are wrong, this is good or this is bad, you shouldn't have done so". We lard our speech with judgments like "normal" or "abnormal" and judge ourselves and others according to the moral values of our time and our culture. Our judgments very often turn us into faultfinders and moralists. To sum up, we call those judgments; **moralistic judgments or judgement based on right and wrong.**

If we judge actions – our own and others – using criteria that have to do with needs and values, we ask ourselves; which needs are met and which needs are not met by this action. We tell others which of our needs are being met or not. The question we ask, and whose answer forms the basis for our judgment is:

"Does this action meet needs or not".

This way of judging we call **value judgments or judgments based on needs.**

We are judging what we and others are doing all the time. If our judgments are based on ideas about right and wrong we will express ourselves differently than if they are based on needs. The consequences of what we say or do will probably also differ.

1. Rosenberg, Marshall (2003), Life-Enriching Education: Nonviolent Communication Helps Schools Improve Performance, Reduce Conflict and Enhance Relationships. PuddleDancer Press.

Reflection

During one period of my life I used to call myself and others "damn cowards". This kind of judgment indicates that I walked around with ideas about how I and others should behave, what we ought to dare to do and how. I assumed that some actions were right and others were wrong.

At one occasion I was extremely disappointed with my friend Peter, and a specific thing he had done. I was irritated, bitter and sore and expressed strong judgments, not only in my head, but also when I talked about him. I told one of my other friends about what was alive in me. Among other labels, I called Peter "a damn coward". My friend listened and surfed with me on my inner "wave of emotions" and once in a while he made a guess which needs of mine that were not being met.

After a while I connected on a deep level with my need for support and my longing for someone to be there for me when I needed it the most. There was so much hidden behind the label "damn coward" that I started crying and continued to do so – suddenly soft instead of tough and hard. My sadness came from all the times when I and others had chosen to withdraw instead of standing up for what we believed in, out of fear of not being accepted or loved.

28

Since that time I have very seldom used the judgment "coward". In situations, where I before would have used it, I today usually connect with how very much I value support and integrity and the fact that I always have a choice of what kind of judgments I want to use, judgments based on right and wrong or judgments based on needs. In the situation with Peter whom I called "damn coward" I might have said to myself:

It's absolutely impossible to trust him. He always lets me down. It's a lot better, if I do whatever has to be done myself, as he has no intention to support anyone else; he thinks only of himself.

If I then, based on that thought made a judgment of my own needs and what I wanted to do to have them met, I could end up with something like:

I'm so darn disappointed, Peter had promised to finish the report and now he comes, two days after the deadline, and tells me he does not want to do the part he promised to do. I have a need for mutual respect in order to put my trust in cooperation in general and I have such a longing for support.

When my judgments are based on needs, I thereby might connect to other unmet needs. If I extend this, I can use my judgment to find out what I want to request from myself, Peter or someone else. Thereby I hopefully won't end up at a dead end, which is usually the case when we use judgments based on "right" and "wrong".

Key Differentiation 29

"Punishments" versus "Consequences"

29

When we talk about **punishments** we refer to a conscious action someone takes, in order to make others understand that they have done "wrong". Or, the opposite, rewards that we give others to show them that we think they are "right". Withholding rewards is also a kind of punishment. A punishment is *executed* by someone and is an active action.

When we talk about **consequences** of our actions we refer to something that happens due to the law of nature. A consequence *occurs* as a result of something we do, on purpose or accidentally. Consequences may or may not meet needs.

It is quite common that the word consequence is used as if it is synonymous with punishment – which we don't think it is – or it is even used to hide the fact that a punishment has been or will be imposed on someone; you punish someone but do not really want to admit it. This linguistic use of the word consequence might be a result of the system we live in, where both punishments and rewards are considered absolutely necessary for the system to function.

It is therefore not surprising that punishments are seen as logical and "natural" consequences when someone has done something "wrong" and that rewards are seen as an equally logical and "natural" consequence when someone has done something "right".

We may say or hear sentences like:

"This is just the consequences of your behavior" or, *"When he sees the consequences he will understand"* although we in fact refer to punishments we or someone else is going to impose.

When we differentiate between punishments and consequences, we see consequences as something natural, resulting from our actions. By "natural" we mean that the consequence of what we do is inevitable; a basketball tossed with a certain speed and angle will hit the basket from above and pass through. A fragile crystal glass will break if we drop it onto the floor, from a specific height and if the floor is of a certain hardness.

It is not a reward for the basketball to go through the basket, and it is not a punishment for the glass if it breaks, it is a consequence. But if we give a gold medal to the person tossing the basketball, than that's a reward, and it's probably heard as a punishment if we grab the person dropping the glass by the arm and say:

"What have you done? Go to your room".

If we focus on the consequences when someone has dropped a glass we would say something like:

"Oh dear, don't move, I don't want you to step on the broken glass, I'll get the vacuum cleaner."

Then maybe I decide that I want to tell the other what I feel now when the glass is broken. Perhaps I don't care about it at all, but it might also be that I'm sad because I want us to be careful with our things.

29

Key Differentiation 30

"Weakness" versus "Vulnerability"

30

When we perceive it as a sign of **weakness** to show feelings, we usually have an inner image of a less capable person. We might even think that this is a person we don't have to take into account. We might also start treating him or her as a child, in ways that prevent them from taking personal responsibility. If we have gotten the idea that the person is so weak that he or she can't handle reality we might even start withholding information.

If we perceive it as a sign of strength to show ones feelings and to show **vulnerability**, it is easier for us to show respect and listen to another person. One of the reasons the giraffe is sometimes used as a symbol for NVC is its long vulnerable neck.

In this case we can say that the difference lies in the eye of the beholder; how we perceive and react to people who openly show their feelings. Sometimes we hear people say that they don't want to talk about their feelings and needs, because they don't want to be considered weak. Maybe they have been raised in a system where it is considered a sign of weakness to have emotions and that "only chicks cry".

Often their basic attitudes are:
- You are strong if you can harbor your feelings without talking to others about them.
- A person talking about feelings and needs shows weakness.
- You can't trust a person who shows weakness, especially not if "there is a storm brewing".

We regard it as valuable to be in touch with one's feelings since we think feelings are an important part of our inner system, signaling whether our needs are being met or not. We all have these kinds of "built-in signals" even if we show them on the outside in varying degrees and in different ways.

When we are "honest" – as we use the word honest – we are open about our feelings and needs with ourselves and with others. We tell about the things that arouse our feelings and about needs we have that are – or are not – being met.

Reflection

For many years I was struggling with my own reactions when other people showed and acted out their feeling. I was carrying a heavy load of exhortations to "keep oneself in check". To keep one's temper was a sign of control and strength.

30

Emotional outbursts – including exuberant joy – were signs of weakness. I can't remember ever having heard about vulnerability, but I do remember having been labeled "hypersensitive" if I, on rare occasions, reacted more strongly than the norm, and showed it.

I think about all of this as I watch a Japanese banker, sitting in the TV-studio, in the full glare of publicity, crying uncontrollably when he realizes the result of a "mistake" he made. How unlike our accustomed way to show our feelings. In one culture it is absolutely okay for a man to show his feelings, in another it is not. During one period in time it is okay, in the next it may be regarded as a sign of weakness.

Perhaps the crying Japanese banker will give others the courage to show their feelings and their vulnerability? I find that thought hopeful[1].

---

1. See also Key Differentiation 9.

Key Differentiation 31

"External Motivation" versus "Inner Motivation"

31

We talk about **external motivation** when our actions are motivated by a wish to be rewarded or to avoid punishments.

Our main motivation is to make others happy and satisfied, or to, in the long run, share some of the special privileges given to people who comply and do as they are told.

When our driving force and motivation comes from within we talk about **inner motivation.** This motivation comes from a desire to meet needs if we choose to, and if we have a choice how to do it and when.

The difference between inner and external motivation can also be described as the difference between intrinsic satisfaction and extrinsic rewards. When we are motivated by an inner desire to meet needs the mere fact that a need is met will motivate us to continue meeting needs. We want to keep our inner motivation alive and vivid and may thereby generate more energy than we need which we can then share with others.

When our driving force comes from a desire for extrinsic rewards, we leave our well-being to the arbitrariness of others; we may or may not be rewarded. In this situation we often increase our efforts, step by step, until we have totally lost all our motivation.

Reflection

I often think about inner and external motivation in connection with the everlasting discussions of grades.

There are people who are of the opinion that children will never ever learn anything at all, if we do not give them extrinsic rewards. The rewards are necessary in order to make the children exert themselves. Which implicitly means *"children have no inner motivation to learn new things"* a thought – according to my experience – contradicted by the march of civilization.

It seems as if we have an irresistible longing to meet our needs – curiosity included. My experiences with children have also convinced me that they, already very early in life, are driven by a desire to investigate and to find out. Even after some years in school the question "Why?" can still be the most frequently asked question.

But, something happens on their way to adulthood. The inner motivation is supplemented with – and sometimes replaced by – an external motivation, in the form of grades, monetary rewards for excellence or a wish for future high social status.

Students drop subjects if they do not trust they will come out well, whether they are interested in the topic or not, and this trend continues when they enter working life.

Many people choose lives and professional careers in search of money and status, however boring and soul suffocating they find it.

Also high-ranking people at the very top of our hierarchical system "need" extra external rewards in the form of bonuses and fringe benefits to be motivated do the job they have already been paid for through their monthly salary.

31

I dream of schools with a philosophy of teaching based on and supportive of children's inherent curiosity and wish to understand life.

I do not want to imply that my goal is to do away with testing and evaluating in our schools, but in my "dream school" the tests are given at the beginning of every learning period – from preschool to university – so that teachers can evaluate the level of knowledge for each individual in order to support each and every one in filling in the gaps.

Key Differentiation 32

"Freedom of Choice" versus "Dependence"

32

To do just the opposite is also a form of imitation.

G.C.LICHTENBERG[1]

What we call acting out of **freedom of choice** is when we choose to act according to our needs, and at the same time taking full responsibility for our actions. We might make requests of others to help us meet our needs, aware that we seldom will have them met on our own as many of our needs are related to community and reciprocity. We make sure to not try to meet our needs at someone else's expense.

If we act on the basis of **dependence**, we might believe that our feelings are caused by what others are doing or saying and that we are responsible for their feelings. In this case we can only be satiesfied if others act in a certain way.

Acting with freedom of choice, we let go of the idea that we cause the feelings others have. Something we do or say may *trigger* feelings in others, but we do *not* cause them. To have freedom of choice does not mean that we ignore others and just think about ourselves. On the contrary, our free will helps us to do things that contribute to our wellbeing, for example by meeting the needs of others.

Our free will also allows us to choose what to do and how, and to abstain from doing things not in harmony with our needs.

If we, on the other hand, live with the notion that we are responsible for each other's feelings, there are two different ways to

---

1. "To do just the opposite is also a form of imitation." Lichtenberg, G.C (1764 – 99). "Lichtenberg, G.C (1764 – 99). From Aphorisms (1990) translated and introduced by R.J. Hollingdale. Penguin Books.

relate to others: Either we submit – as we think we are responsible for what others are feeling – or we rebel and refuse to care about the feelings and needs of others. Those who submit often do it to avoid punishment and they disclaim any responsibility, as they "only did what they were told to do."

A person rebelling wants to show that he or she can do whatever they want – without considering needs – that one does not have to do as one is told. It may be experienced as some kind of "freedom" - but freedom based on rebellion has other driving forces than freedom of choice.

Most of us receive early in life a solid training in obedience and submission. We have also heard parents or teachers express their joy or their grief over something a six-year-old has done: *"Oh, now I am really happy when you do as daddy says",*

or:

"Now mum is very sad, I told you to pick up the toys".

The child is more or less consistently taught that the parent's feelings depend on something the child did or did not do. Very often the parents also think that is the case, i.e. they think their feelings are caused by the child. This has been part of our cultural education for several thousand years.

Many react by submitting; others rebel and take every chance to show their "freedom". The more persistent the parent is in making the child obey, the more opportunities the child will have to rebel and experience some kind of "freedom" – a freedom very different from what we are referring to when we use the word. The "freedom" achieved by rebelling is closely akin to submission, just another side of dependence.

32

If we want to encourage freedom of choice it helps if people around us also experience freedom to choose.

Reflection

I am often surprised at how much I learn from my three-year-old about communicating. He did not want to brush his teeth and we tried to protect his oral health in all ways possible. During this time he very often used the word "together" and one evening when his father and I were brushing our teeth his father said:

"Mother is brushing her teeth, father is brushing his teeth, Neo is brushing his teeth, and we are together.

Neo looked at him and said quietly:

"Mother is brushing her teeth, father is brushing his teeth, Neo is not brushing his teeth, and we are still together."

He was aware that he "belonged" and that he was free to choose. He knew he did not have to submit to belong. We had to find other ways to protect his teeth, than alluding to his need for community.

I think the difference between freedom of choice and dependence - and submission or rebellion - is obvious for many of us. We can feel our inner motivation, even if we do not use exactly those words. When we obey or rebel we have given up our freedom and perceive ourselves as directed by either internal or external expectations.

When we submit, we often do it for fear of punishment, to avoid guilt or shame, or because we cannot see that we have a choice, we simply think it is our duty. Also when rebelling we are influenced by what is happening around us. We want to show that we are free in relation to demands we think are placed on us. Those demands - whether fictional or real – make it important for us to break existing standards, not because we like what we are doing when we rebel, but because the freedom we experience, while doing it, is so obvious. This kind of "freedom" has its limitations and therefore has to be manifested over and over again. When we, on the other hand, experience genuine freedom, our focus is on needs - how our needs and the needs of others can be met.[2]

---

2. You can read more in Nonviolent Communication, a language of life, by Marshall Rosenberg. Puddle Dancer Press. Chapters 5, 11 and 12.

Key Differentiation 33

"Dependence or Independence" versus "Interdependence"

33

Dependence: When our actions are based on thoughts that we are dependent, we do not see that we have any choice but to do what we think others expect of us. These thoughts are nourished by the idea that some people are inferior, others superior, and those inferior are dependent to those superior and their capriciousness. We associate dependence with powerlessness.

Independence: Sometimes we tell ourselves we are completely independent of others. We rebel against the notion that some are inferior and others are superior and we cannot see that we depend on others or on the environment. We associate independence with self-sufficiency.

Interdependence: When we see that we are mutually dependent, we have realized that whatever we do or refrain from doing, will have an impact on others and on the environment. Interdependence means we respect our own needs as well as the needs of others.

We act out of free will without any thought of inferiority or superiority, punishments or rewards, fully aware of our interdependence with our surroundings. We can see how we are all connected by giving and receiving, and that our relation to ourselves is based on those connections.

While growing up, most of us tend to gradually experience individual freedom. We may later be very keen to nurture and retain this freedom, maybe at the expense of reciprocity. For others the connection with this freedom may be frightening as it also means that they recognize their responsibility for the choices they make.

As soon as we realize that we are interdependent we see that whatever we do, we affect and are affected by others and the environment. When we think we are independent we do not take this aspect of life into account. If we think we are dependent, we cannot see that we are free, and act without reflecting over how our actions may affect others and the environment.

Reflection

I have made it a habit to now and then suggest a "silent dining table", where we eat in silence when attending a seminar, conference or spending a prolonged time with others. This is not to avoid contact – on the contrary. The silence allows me to connect with whatever else feels important to me. Sometimes I end up alone at the table, but often a few others join me at the table in silence.

These moments help me to get in contact with mutuality, the interdependence I am in and can celebrate internally as I eat in silence.

I can begin by looking around at all the other people who, at **33** this moment, are eating their meal with me. We are all, at this moment, so dependent upon what other people – often worldwide – have contributed to the food we are eating.

My thoughts can start with the kitchen staff that prepared the meal – then expand to the people who transported the ingredients to the kitchen. Maybe I begin to wonder how the driver – possibly driving under difficult road conditions to transport vegetables from southern Europe – has contributed to my meal. I also think about how the money I pay for my food may help the driver realize his or her dreams. I send grateful thoughts, mixed with some concern and worry – to the grower of the vegetables – and wonder if he has sprayed the plants with pesticides. I visualize the farmers toiling from early morning until late at night regardless of weather conditions. I imagine how he or she makes sure the seeds get planted, how the crop grows, gets weeded when necessary and how the farmer sprays with pesticides if needed - likely to be hazardous to his health - to prevent bugs and mold from ruining the crop. My thoughts wander to the factory worker who has prepared and packaged the peppercorns later used to enhance the taste of my food, to the tea leaf picker who has collected the leaves for my cup of tea, to the person who has swept up the sundried sea salt and to the one who has endured the heat necessary to melt the metal for the manufacturing of the fork I hold in my hand.

A "simple plate of food" can provide us with a journey around the world as well as nutrition and yummy food – as it reminds us of our interdependence, on each other and on nature.

Key Differentiation 34

"Appreciation" versus "Approval"

34

To express **appreciation** is a way to celebrate and tell some-one that something he or she said or did not say, met our needs. Appreciations - as the word is used in NVC – consists of an observation, a pleasant feeling, and a need that has been met. Appreciations are often nourishing for the recipient as well as for the sender.

Approval, praise and compliments are kinds of rewards based on the concept of "right and wrong", "normal" and "abnormal". Those rewards contain judgments and may establish an – often devastating - addiction to approval from others, thereby sometimes contributing to people disregarding their own needs in favor of the needs of others.

One important difference between appreciation and approval lies in the intent. When we give appreciation our intention is to cel-ebrate needs met, to share the joy we feel with the people who made the difference. We tell others what actions of theirs made our life more wonderful.

The intention of giving compliments and praise may be to "make" the other person repeat something that pleased us, and or to make them act, in a special way, to be loved and approved by us. We judge whether they are good, normal, smart or perfect; we describe

what they "are". The praise and approval is based on our perception of "right" and "wrong" and we grant ourselves the liberty to act as judges. Even when the judgment is "positive", it is still a judgment based on the concept of "right and wrong".

Reflection

34

Many people seem to have taken it on themselves to help others build self-confidence by telling them that they are clever, beautiful, gifted or amiable.

To hear this type of judgment from others poses a risk that – instead of feeling acceptance, love or respect for oneself – one gets more and more dependent upon the approval of others in order to feel good. One perhaps even starts putting on pressure to always match up to the judgments, demanding from oneself to always be "smart", "nice" or "intelligent", demands that easily become overwhelming and may lead to self-contempt.

I have been involved with people who have given me lots of compliments. I understand now that they praised my ability to do this or that, as a strategy to make me do more and to do it even better next time. And I did just that, as a strategy to be seen, to experience fellowship or to be loved.

"You are so good at doing this. Will you please come tomorrow night and help me fix it?"

Month after month, year after year. Until the judgments were not even positive anymore, they were more like:

"Weren't you supposed to have fixed this yesterday, I thought we had agreed that this is your responsibility. And now you haven't done it, you just ignored it. I can't trust you anymore."

So, what was initially meant as an appreciation – although in the form of a judgment – changed into demands and damaged relationships.

I think about what a difference it would have made had the appreciation been given to me as the joyful feelings and needs my actions could contribute to – or already had contributed to – if the person had said something like:

"I just want to tell you how wonderful it is that you know how to wallpaper a room. I saw the wallpapering you did at Peter's place and thought it would be nice to make some changes in my house with my birthday at hand. The mere thought of engaging someone I'm not acquainted with makes me miserable. The planning is much more convenient if the two of us can do it together, so I wonder if you are willing to come and help me paper one of the walls in my dining room."

This could be an attempt to manipulate me by soft soaping me. I can't be quite sure of the intention until I see how the other person reacts if I say "no" to their request. Even if the other person mentions both feelings and needs there is no guarantee that it is an honest appreciation. I can try to find out whether it is or not, by simply saying:

"So, I hear that it would really be helpful for you if I came to your place and helped wallpaper your dining room before your birthday, and I hear you say that you appreciated the work I did at Peter's place. This month and next I'm very busy and have other things I want to do. How is it for you to hear me say that?"

"It's absolutely OK, I just wanted you to know that I liked what you did at Peter's place, and I will celebrate my birthday again next year, so perhaps I'll ask you again later."

If that's the answer, I feel safe that the appreciation was sincere and I can celebrate that I can contribute to others when I choose to.

Key Differentiation 35

"Stimulus" versus "Cause"

35

When we talk about feelings in NVC it is often clarifying to distinguish between what stimulates and what causes the feeling.

Stimulus: something we observe. We hear someone say or do something that "triggers" our feelings and reminds us of needs we have that are or are not being met. Our thoughts and sometimes what we call our "inner voice" also function as triggers.

Cause: our needs. When practicing NVC we seek the cause of our feelings among our universal needs, needs we share with every human being and partly with all other living creatures. Our feelings change constantly, depending on whether our needs are met or not and how we approach them.

There is reason for us to look closer at the difference between stimulus and cause. Stimuli sometimes "mess it up" for us and become a real challenge. But in most cases they help us "locate the cause," to find the underlying need, to help us act to have the need met, instead of turning on the "messenger". Stimuli are signals affecting our senses; light stimulating the optic nerve and sound stimulating the auditory nerve.

When we practice NVC we usually exemplify this difference by describing what someone is saying or doing – what we can observe – as stimuli. Our reaction to what we observe is due to or caused by our needs. If the stimulus is a hissing snake, we may react with fear, caused by our need for protection and security, or

with amazement over the wonders of nature.

On the other hand, if the stimulus is a yodeling neighbor, we may react with frustration, caused by our need for serenity, tranquility and harmony. Or, our reaction to exactly the same stimulus may also be one of joy, caused by our need for celebration and to have fun. Other people's behavior may be stimuli for our reactions, but it is our needs, that are the cause. This also explains why one and the same stimulus can result in diametrically different reactions – not only among different people, but also for the same individual. When our needs are met we react with certain feelings and if they are not met we react in a different way.

35

When practicing NVC we talk sometimes about "inner Jackals" meaning our inner voices and thoughts. The most frequent thoughts are judgments, labels, "ought to's" and musts. These "inner Jackals" may, as with other voices we have, act as stimuli. When we think that someone is reckless it stimulates our anger, and the anger may in turn be caused by the fact that our need of care, for example, is not currently being met.

As soon as we translate the "inner Jackals" into feelings and needs, our anger usually turns into sadness or anxiety, caused by our needs. Looked at in this way, it is perhaps more of a philosophical question whether the thought leading to anger is a stimulus or a cause. Here, we confine ourselves to pointing out that there is a connection.

Reflection

My friend Eva, working as a stand-in nurse, was asked: *"Do you want to make the coffee for our breaks next week?"* The question made her happy. She was new on the job and had found it difficult to feel part of the group. She thanked the person asking her about making the coffee and said she was happy as the question was like an invitation to be part of the group.

Sara, another friend of mine, called me, very frustrated, and told me a very similar story. She was also new on her job and was asked pretty much the same question as Eva. Sara worked as a doctor and when I had listened to her upset feelings for a while, it became clear that her need to be seen – contrary to Eva's – was not being met.

"They should understand how busy I am! And they should understand what it is like to be new to the job and have all this responsibility for things I hardly know how they work! Do I have to explain everything to them?"

As I hear Sara say "should understand" I can see the link between her thoughts and her outrage.

Eva and Sara have been through almost exactly the same situations. Eva feels happy, Sara frustrated. Eva wanted to be seen and included in the group, Sara wanted to be seen and respected, for how hard it is to come into a new workplace. Both had the same need - to be seen - and yet their reactions differed as a result of how they felt about the situation and what needs were most alive in them at the time. The stimulus was the same: *"Do you want to make the coffee next week?"*

Imagine that you are at a party and Niclas – someone you know just briefly – catches a glimpse of you, makes a wry face, turns around and walks away.

What are your feelings? It depends of course on your thoughts and what you think is happening in Niclas and the needs you may have hoped to meet when you first saw him. If you had been looking forward to seeing Niclas, hoping it was the same for him, you might feel scared, disappointed or sad. If you absolutely did not want to see him because of something that had happened in the last few days, you may feel relieved because he does not seem to want to connect with you either. So his actual behavior, to make a face and go the other way, was not the cause of your emotions. His face stimulated feelings *connected* to your thoughts and *caused* by your needs.

One of my friends sent me the letter below, describing experiences I think clarifies the difference between stimulus and cause.

"My father and I only have contact with one another via cellphone. Periodically I have severed connections with him completely as I did not enjoy the way we connected.

A major irritation for me has been that he calls me at hours I **35** *don't like. He often calls when he has been drinking alcohol and then either early in the morning, before he falls asleep, around six, or at night, around two when he wants to talk. Some years ago my a friend of mine had an accident and tried to call me from the hospital late at night. I did not answer. I was asleep and had the cell phone on silent mode because my dad had called me several nights in a row and woke me up. My irritation over the fact that he did not respect my request to call in the daytime was already great and grew after this. I thought he was disrespectful, selfish and clearly proving that he really did not care about me. Time passed and suddenly three weeks, without contact had passed. I had called him several times in the last few days, but his cell phone was switched off. My concern grew that something serious had happened.*

I worried that the police would call to inform me that they had found him dead. Then one night I was awakened at 3 am by my cellphone and on the display I read, Dad. This time I was not annoyed but relieved and happy. It became clear to me that it was not the time he called me that caused my irritation but all the thoughts I had about why he did it. Dad's choice to call me late at night or early in the morning had only stimulated these thoughts and my irritation. I could see that my need for rest, respect and caring was the underlying cause of my emotions. When I later spoke to dad about this it was so much easier for me to connect - because I had seen this difference."

Key Differentiation 36

"Compromise" versus "Shift"

Friendship is composed of a single soul inhabiting two bodies.
- ARISTOTELSES

36

When we **compromise** we focus on finding a solution by seeing what each one is willing to give up in order to gain something. Compromise can be looked upon as a trade-off between sometimes unequal parties. Even if compromises sometimes work, often no one is really happy with the results.

In order to achieve a **shift** we focus on needs. We pay attention to all parties' needs, before trying to find a solution in which these needs are taken into account. We trust that people want to cooperate when they can do so voluntarily without anyone forcing them. The shift itself happens when everybody involved can let go of their original strategies in favor of strategies where everybody's needs may be met and where both parties are satisfied with the alternative strategy.

When we connect to the needs of others there may be a shift within us as soon as we realize in what way we can contribute to them if we say "yes" to their request. And sometimes it is not until both parties have expressed and heard each other's needs that a shift may occur. With the needs of both parties "on the table" it is usually easy to find strategies that meet as many of the needs presented as possible.

A friend, whom I had not met for a long time, called me and asked if we could meet for coffee. I was tired and really needed to rest, so I hesitated. As I had lately experienced how profoundly honesty and empathy could make things shift, I decided to be honest. At the same time I also told him that my answer might change if he could tell me why it was important for him that we do something together.

When I listened to him and how important it was for him to experience community I also connected to my wish to contribute to that. That gave me the energy I had thought was possible to get only by resting. Now it was easy for me to choose coffee instead of rest, as it became clear to me what it meant to us both.

Reflection

A shift like this differs from a compromise. In a compromise I partly give up or agree to do something the other person asks me to do, though I don't want to, and under the condition that the other person is willing to do something similar for me. "I scratch your back, and you scratch mine."

36

The shift I describe above is due to both of us having connected to needs and from a genuine wish to enrich life. With this kind of shift, no one is giving up or giving in against their will. I never thought I was "helping out" or that he now owed me a debt of gratitude. We went to a coffee shop together and it meant a lot for me to be able to contribute and to share some valuable moments with a person who meant a lot to me.

Shifts like this do not come with a hidden "price tag," arriving like a bill in the mailbox when least expected. On the contrary, it deepens the connection through the dialogue around feelings and needs that led to the shift.

Another one of my friends told me how nearly every weekend she and her ex- boyfriend ended up in the same locked positions. It could go like this.

"I wanted us to take it easy and just spend a relaxed weekend together just the two of us. He wanted us to party with friends both Friday and Saturday. And to avoid ending up in a shouting match we compromised. Partying on Friday, relaxing at home on Saturday. We were both uncomfortable doing what the other wanted to do. Neither of us enjoyed doing what we did not want to do. So whatever we were doing one of us was not happy. And, as you know, we finally broke up. Had we instead planned our weekends after having listened to each other's feelings and needs, I think both of us might have experienced a shift. We would not have tried the compromise. Instead we perhaps could have found a third, alternative way meeting both his and my needs. And perhaps I would have loved to party on Fridays, had I understood the beautiful needs my ex-boyfriend wanted to meet with that strategy. And perhaps he would have loved to stay at home Saturdays, had he understood mine."

Key Differentiation 37

"Acts that Serve Life" versus "Acts that Distance Us From Life"

37

People are very scared of spending so much of their lives having to give when it is not from the heart.

MARSHALL ROSENBERG[1]

When we talk about **acts that serve life** our focus is on meeting universal needs when we act and when we communicate. We want to listen emphatically and express ourselves honestly. When we connect to other human beings and with the rest of creation, we want to act taking all needs into consideration. Our power comes from our desire to meet needs.

When we talk about **acts that distance us from life** we refer to things we do because we tell ourselves that "one has to do this" or "one ought to do that". We strive to do what is "right" and avoid doing what is "wrong". When our focus is on judgments like these and on the rewards we think we deserve, there is an obvious risk that we distance ourselves from life. Perhaps we act without any understanding of the consequences when our power comes from a longing "to please" or from a wish to avoid penalties.

Sometimes we are not aware of whether our actions are serving life or not, or if they are distancing us. Without realizing it, many things we do do serve life, but sadly enough many of our actions actually distance us from life. From the outside our actions may

1. Rosenberg, Marshall (2005), Being me, loving you, A Practical Guide to Extraordinary Relationships. Puddle Dancer Press.

159

look identical. What differs is why we do what we do. Irrespective of where our driving force comes from - from the outside or from within – our willingness to meet needs is essential – our needs and the needs of others. If we act without having connected to needs there is a risk that we stop acts that serve life as soon as outer rewards or threats of punishments are no longer present.

Many of us struggled to get good grades in school or to win competitions, but then gave up completely when outer rewards did not come as expected.

Reflection

Years ago, the folktale about the shepherd boy and the wolf was told in our schools. The boy had been tending the sheep all day and was bored. He came up with an idea to get some company. He cried out as loud as he could:

"The wolf is coming! The wolf is coming!"

People from a neighboring village came to his rescue, only to find they had been fooled. The shepherd boy laughed and thought it was a funny joke. The next day he repeated it:

"The wolf is coming! The wolf is coming!"

And as in the day before, people came running to his aid, only to find the boy laughing at his joke. The third day, the wolf really did come! Again the boy cried "The wolf is coming! The wolf is coming! This time no one came to rescue the boy and his sheep. This folktale served as an example and warning about what happens if we "cry for help" without due cause.

37

It is often challenging to continue listening when someone uses the same empty threats - or more or less obvious "cries for help" - over and over again. When I was a child my mother often threatened to pack her trunk and leave. Eventually everyone stopped listening to her. The way she communicated her longing for support and to be loved made her chances to get what she wanted less and less likely. I know that I, and probably the rest of my family, began to shut ourselves off from her. We reacted to her "cry for help" as the villagers did to the shepherd boy, we stopped listening. Had we had the ability to listen in a life serving way, we could have heard her deeper needs. We could have heard what she was longing for and tried to communicate with her recurring threats. Had she been aware of alternative ways to connect and get support to meet her needs, she could have chosen other ways to express herself.

Key Differentiation 38

"Demanding" versus "Persisiting"

38

When we **demand** to have our needs met, we do not take into consideration that others also want to decide for themselves what to do. A person making demands wants to see something specific happen without taking into account how it affects others.

With **persisting** we mean staying connected to our needs without punishing persons who say "no" to our requests. We stay connected and continue our dialogue until everyone's needs are included.

Reflection

Tindra, a three-year-old girl, and her father were visiting her grandmother. The father later described what took place as one of the most beautiful examples of persisting that he had experienced. Tindra's two older cousins had been allowed to join their grandfather in his studio to watch him painting.

She was very curious and wanted to see what grandpa and the cousins were doing. She pulled on her father's pants and wanted him to go with her to the studio as she was anxious about going there on her own. Her father was busy talking to her grandmother and did not want the conversation to be interrupted. Tindra repeatedly said that she wanted to join her cousins in the studio and her father answered that he did not want to go. He said it more than once and with ever stronger emphasis:

"NO, I DON'T WANT TO!"

Tindra persisted and her father tried to recall what he had learned about using feelings and needs when one is connecting to people we usually label "children." He had heard someone say something like this in a similar situation:

"Tell her what you do want, instead of saying what you don't want. Or try to understand why she wants you to join her and perhaps that will affect your choice."

38

He turned to Tindra and said:

"Tindra, I guess that you want us to go together to grandpa's studio and that you are curious and want to know what grandpa and your cousins are doing. But I actually want to stay here and talk to grandma."

Hearing that, Tindra went to the stairs leading to the studio and called to her cousins as loud as she could:

"Come here, because I want to be with you and see what you are doing!"

To me this story is a powerful example of how we can persist and hold on to our request, without demanding. Tindra had her need for community met and her father could continue talking to his mother.

I often see people giving up their needs and requests as soon as they hear a "no." I also see many people trying to make demands. In both cases the result is that only one person has their needs met, not at all like what happened between Tindra and her father.

I often think about a relationship I was in where I did not stand up for my needs, something I still mourn a lot. The relationship was with a man who was very important to me. His girlfriend "was jealous" of me and asked me to not contact him anymore. As I got stuck in thoughts of being selfish or obnoxious, which I found uncomfortable, I said "yes" to her wish.

Now, knowing how my "yes" made me feel and the tragic outcome that was to come, I wish I had said something like this instead:

"Our relationship is so important to me that I would love to continue seeing him. At the same time I hear that you don't want us to meet and guess there are several important needs you want to meet by that. Could we try to find out together how to go on from here in a way that functions for all of us?"

We had not had any contact at all when a year later I learned that their relationship had ended and that my friend had committed suicide. In the midst of my grief it became very clear to me how important it would have been for me to stand up for my need for connection – some kind of contact – and that I could have done so without demanding. I could have shown him that I wanted to be there for him. Maybe it would have made a difference.

Key Differentiation 39

"Love as a Feeling" versus "Love as a Need"

39

The word love is used to describe feelings as well as needs; therefore it may contribute to clarity in our communication if we are aware of, and clear about, how we use the word.

When talking about **love as a feeling** we use words describing feelings like happy, glad, delighted, or overwhelmed. And as with other feelings they are by nature signals telling us that one or more of our needs are being met at that moment. Two minutes later the feeling might change.

When talking about **love as a need**, we are referring to something universal and constant. All human beings are born with the same universal needs and love is one of them. We often associate

the need for love with other needs; intimacy, trust, belonging, acceptance, respect, emotional safety and care.

When Marshall Rosenberg talks about love and to love, he often answers the question "do you love me?" by saying "when?" to highlight the difference between using the word as a feeling and as a need. If the person asking wants to know what the other is feeling, the answer may change from one moment to the next. Exuberant happiness can be exchanged for deepest grief.

Reflection

So, what do we mean when we talk about love and to love? If I ask someone if he or she loves me, is it then unambiguous if I get a "yes" or a "no" as an answer? And if my partner answers "Yes, of course I love you" what has he or she actually told me? If I want to know what he or she – right now – feels in relation to me and what needs are met, I could have asked exactly that.

But we seldom put our questions like that, perhaps for fear of the response, perhaps because we never thought it could deepen our connection if we really put "present needs on the table." In the musical "Fiddler on the roof" Tevye asks his wife Golde:

"Do you love me?"

She looks at him in surprise and says:

39

"Do I love you? With our daughters getting married and this trouble in the town? You are upset, you are worn out. Go inside, go lie down!"

But Tevye insists and asks again:

"Do you love me?"

Golde answers:

"For twenty-five years I have washed your clothes, cooked your meals, cleaned your house. Given you children, milked the cow. After twenty-five years, why talk about love right now? For twenty-five years I have lived with you. Fought you, starved with you. For twenty-five years my bed is yours. If that's not love, what is? I suppose I love you and after twenty-five years it's nice to know."

In another tale, a woman asked her husband the same question:

"Do you love me?"

His answer was, according to the tall story:

"I told you so when we got married and if there is a change I'll let you know."

I have had divided feelings about his answer but I can see that there is something beautiful in his approach. The beauty - as I see it - lies in his trust that if you stay in a relationship that is a sign of some kind of love. Love is than something you "live" rather than something you talk about. Although it may be comforting to hear and to put love into words, we also value the fact that the other person has stayed in the relationship and we can take that as a sign that his or her needs for love are being met. If those needs are not being met the couple either breaks up or begins to take their needs seriously and together finds new strategies to meet their need for love. Striving to meet needs is a strong motivator for all of us.

Key Differentiation 40

"Natural" versus "Habitual"

40

Something **natural** describes laws of nature and congenital qualities like our connection to our needs.

When we talk about something as **habitual** we refer to things that have been learned; our language, how we express ourselves, the standards and cultural patterns we follow.

We sometimes jokingly call it "the marinade we are swimming in" to illustrate how that which is habitual easily becomes as self-evident as the air we breathe. We may continue to swim in our marinade, without discovering that there is a natural ocean surrounding our tiny jar of marinade.

Since what is habitual is something we have learned, we can choose to change it. When we act habitually we often call our actions "natural".

Many expressions we use may contribute to the confusion regarding these concepts. We can for example hear someone say, *"Naturally I got angry when I heard him call me chubby"* or *"Isn't it natural that fathers go to work and mothers stay at home taking care of the children."* But it is not that simple. What is regarded as "natural" in one culture is "unnatural" in another.

We learn that there is a "right way" to relate to others and accept it as a matter of fact. We have only come in contact with a rather limited variety of people; what they look like, how they treat one another and how they address each other. As a consequence we name phenomenon we recognize as "natural", although they are often "habitual". Life becomes so much easier if we act according to manners and customs; practicing what is "normal and natural" in the culture where we live. We also regard many of our habits as "good habits" and they usually serve us well, as it is something we do regularly and do not have to think about.

But when we think our customs are natural it may be difficult for us to change what we have gotten accustomed to. We easily tell ourselves that what we do is "natural" and use that as an excuse for not changing our behavior. Traditions, habits, customs and practices that we call "natural" and "normal" are usually difficult to change or break.

Our feelings, like hunger for example, are natural and eating is a natural consequence. *What* I do when I feel hungry – and *what* I eat is usually habitual. In our culture we might go to the fridge or call out for pizza if we are hungry. In another culture you might ask someone to kill a rooster when you are hungry.

Our longing for freedom is like our need for food and our other needs, something we are born with and something we are willing to protect as long as possible. But *what* we do to experience freedom can be either natural or habitual or both. Some of us might experience freedom by having a drink, others might take a walk. A third person might start divorce proceedings and a fourth might take a trip around the world with some friends. And someone wants to watch the same TV show as his friends at the day care center.

Reflection

40

During a rather prolonged period, my four-year-old son wanted to watch the TV show "Pokémon". Pokémons are small "animals" or "monsters", small enough to be put in your pocket. A Pokémon cartoon was on one of the TV channels and as I watched it I saw a number of fights, a lot of sarcasm and other forms of violence. I became thoughtful when I realized that the focus in this children's cartoon was on using the right form of attack or preventing attacks from the enemy. The "good team" was of course winning most of the battles. A familiar feature in the marinade we are swimming in.

The next time my son asked if he could watch Pokémon, I being the grown up, used my power to protect him:

"No, I want you to watch something else. ."

His disappointment was bitter and we talked about it a long time without finding a solution. He started whining, and told me that he wanted to watch Pokémon using arguments like *"all the other children at the day care center watch it."* He even threatened to run away from home.

Then one day he to my surprise asked me:

"Mommy, what do you need to change your mind about me watching Pokémon?"

It looked as if he had realized that I had a reason to say "no", that a need of mine made me say "no". We had the most fantastic dialogue, though to start with it was not obvious to me what I needed. I knew I wanted to protect him from violence as much as possible. I also knew my "no" was not meant as a punishment.

But what in fact did I need? Oh yes, I needed trust. Trust that I do what I believe in and trust that I live by my values. It was important to me that what he watched on TV was something he could handle in ways that would not injure him or others.

Consequently I told him how important trust and safety is for me. Then I asked him if he wanted to watch one Pokémon episode together with me so that we could talk afterwards about what needs of his were met and what needs he thought the small *monsters* wanted to meet. He found my suggestion OK, but five minutes later he came back to me and asked:

"Mom, what is a need?"

That was a challenge! How to explain what needs are to my understanding? I had used the word "need" for at least ten years while teaching and in my writings:

"What is this thing called need?"

Finally I found out that needs to my understanding are the innate, natural powers we all have, powers meant to keep us healthy and alive in order to survive as individuals and as a species. Our needs express our wish to continue living and therefore – moment by moment – our feelings signal us about our needs, as the most natural thing in the world.

When I told my son about needs in a way he could grasp, he just giggled and ran off to play, stating as a matter of fact that Pokémons do not have any needs.

40

Key Differentiation 41

"Accomplish" versus "Create"

When we **accomplish**, we are looking for acknowledgement from others that we are right, that we are good, that others like what we are doing and that we are "capable". We listen to judgments from others and to our inner "judge". When we accomplish something we sometimes also compare ourselves with others or with our own previous accomplishments.

When we **create** we are fully aware that our aim is to meet needs; everything from the need of creativity and zest for life to realizing dreams. It can also be about clarifying and elucidating something, so that the insights we have gained may contribute to us and others. In the creation process, we meet those needs, and our own feeling of satisfaction is the acknowledgement we long for.

Many people also express having fun while creating.

In retrospect, this differentiation has become apparent to me when it comes to my own relation to studying.

Reflection

Many years ago I thought that one of my high school teachers had treated me unjustly. I decided to "indeed show the jerk what I can do" I went on to study his subject at the university level. After a great deal of worry and trouble - taking tests and re-taking tests, (resulting in my growing fear of exams) I at last obtained my degree but without feeling any joy at all.

Many years later I went back to the university to study economics. I was interested in studying the driving forces of economy in society for totally different reasons. I pondered the fact that everyone talks about justice, equal rights and how important it is to protect the environment. And still the distribution of the Earth's resources looks the way it does. An incredibly strong desire to understand all this came from within. I wanted to combine knowledge from different areas in a creative way, to find a platform from what researchers had come up with; a platform where I could feel firmly grounded and secure. I wanted to find and clarify causal connections.

41

I was searching for knowledge. I was longing to meet needs of mine and my studies went like clockwork. My fear of exams completely vanished, writing papers was sheer pleasure, and I looked forward to every single lecture and loved to discuss my insights with others.

When I realized the difference between studying in order to accomplish something and studying in order to meet needs, it also made me, as a teacher, search for new ways of teaching in the classroom. I began using a more problem oriented approach. I invited the students – when possible - to articulate issues and problems they themselves were interested in exploring. With my help they searched for knowledge – not necessarily in order to find a solution to the problem but to be able to shed light upon the issue from many different angles.

Key Differentiation 42

"Open Questions" versus "Closed Questions"

42

Open questions are questions we ask when we want to know something we think the other person might have an answer to. It may be about facts or other information, but open questions may also be used when we want to understand what is alive in another person.

Closed questions are questions we ask when we already have a perception of the answer. Closed questions can usually be answered with just "yes" or "no".

When we ask a question, regardless of context, we can influence the answer we get, just by how we formulate the question and to whom we ask it.

This is a well-known phenomenon among those engaged in opinion polls and witness psychology. When we are aware of the fact that *how* we state our questions and the influence it may have on the answer, we can make informed choices when we want to connect to others.

When using NVC we use both open and closed questions. Whatever wording we choose, the *intention* behind us asking is a wish to connect with what is alive in another person.

In NVC we use closed questions when we sense or guess what someone is feeling and needing. We ask to get clarity about which feelings and needs are most alive in another person. The advantage of using closed questions is that they support us in keeping the dialogue around feelings and needs. When we ask closed questions and include what we guess the other is feeling and needing it may sound like this:

"How is it, are you extremely upset because your contact is so important for you?"

If the answer is "yes" our ideas may have been confirmed, but we do not know for sure if we got to know more about what is alive in the other person. In the worst case scenario we have not contributed to connection at all. If we continue asking *closed questions*, this way of questioning may be part of listening empathically. If in this case we instead ask *open questions*, the person may start talking about his or her feelings. Perhaps they start talking about wrongdoings by others and about self-pity or get stuck in thoughts distancing them further from a solution.

When using NVC, our open questions contain the feelings and needs we as questioners want to meet by asking. The mere fact that we pose a question is per se a way to direct. The advantage of using open questions is that the questioner's control is minimized for the benefit of the other person, who can answer more freely.

When we ask open questions the chances increase that we get to know more about the actual feelings in the other person. This makes it easier for us to guess what their unmet need is right now. Perhaps we say:

"I feel a little bit worried and would like to understand, are you willing to tell me more about your feelings now when he has moved out?"

The open question offers the other person a chance to use their own words to tell about feelings, thoughts and perhaps even needs alive in him or her. We may listen emphatically in silence or by guessing what their needs are. If our question is answered in a way that does not reveal any needs – but is more about wrongdoings by others – we can always change our question and use a closed question focusing on feelings and needs alive in the person we are talking to.

42

- By asking closed questions focusing on needs we can achieve the same kind of connection as with open questions.

- Open questions like *"How are you?"* and *"What's the matter?"* are usually used as greetings, as they do not normally lead to responses other than: *"Quite well, how about you?"* or something similar.

Reflection

As a young journalist on a local radio station in the sixties, I was once asked to do a survey with by-passers at the local marketplace. To work this way as a reporter was new and nearly revolutionary at the time. The subject for the day was "mistrust of politicians." In a happy mood and with my microphone poised, I asked the unsuspecting citizens:

"Do you think it's okay that our politicians eat "suffragettes" at the Waldorf Astoria for lunch, at the taxpayers' expense?"

Every single person answered "no". Some thought it was totally wrong. Others were outraged and expressed their contempt. Some looked bewildered but still thought it was wrong.

When I analyzed the answers I got, I came to only one conclusion; I had no idea what people really thought about politicians. They were perhaps familiar with the word "suffragettes" and knew that the word referred to women who fought for the right for women to vote in Britain and the US in the early 20th century. In that case that might have been the reason their answer was "no". Or they could have said no because they thought our taxes should go to more important things than lunches for politicians. Some of them may have said "no" because they thought that the Waldorf Astoria was not good enough for our politicians and that they should eat at more expensive restaurants.

My question was not just a closed one; it was insidiously worded and directed. And perhaps that is not an unusual way to put one's questions. The more aware we become of how important the way we word our questions is for our ability to connect to others, the easier it will be for us to make informed choices both when asking and answering questions.

An extra and serious dimension is added to the saying "What goes around, comes around" where in a scientific test people were shown a short film sequence of two cars colliding[1]. Afterwards half of the participants were asked the following question:

*"At what speed were the cars driving when they **crashed**?"*

The answer was on average 68 km/h, and they also stated that they had observed pieces of broken glass. The other group of participants was asked a slightly different question:

*"At what speed were the cars driving when they **bumped into** each other?"*

In this group the average speed was estimated to be 51 km/h and no one stated that they had seen any broken glass. In a seemingly open question it is obviously sufficient to change a word or two to get a wholly or partially different answer.

---

1. http://utveckling.mastercoach.se 20100415.

42

Group Exercises to Explore Key Differentiations

Purpose of activity:
To deepen the understanding of the Key Differentiations in NVC. Practicing cooperation to get clarity.

Procedure:
Step 1:
- Divide participants into small groups; 3-5 people.

Step 2:
- Every participant chooses one Key Differentiation he or she wants to describe. If you want to make the exercise more challenging you may let someone else in your group make the choice for you. We have added a list of all the Key Differentiations at the end of the exercise. Copy it and cut them out, one Differentiation on each piece of paper. Then draw lots.

Step 3:
- A) Participant one: Take one minute (someone is the time keeper) and describe your understanding of *your* Key Differentiation. You can start by saying: "The difference between X versus Y is ..."; or you agree in advance to use, let's say, one to three sentences or a specific number of words, to describe *your* Key Differentiation.
B) When participant one has used his/her minute the next participant continues and describes her/his understanding of this differentiation. Continue until all participants have told their understanding of this Key Differentiation. Then you start over again with participant two/three/four/five and his/her Key Differentiation.

Continue until all participants have told their understanding of every Key Differentiation in question.

Variation of the above exercise:
- Step 1: As above.
- Step 2: As above.
- Step 3:
- A) Participant X (any one of the group) opposes participant one. When participant one tells his/her understanding of the Key Differentiation in question, X says something like: "I really don't understand why it's so important to differentiate between these two (for example need versus strategy)" In this case the participant is not a person in pain, he/she is only asking for intellectual clarity, and for participant one to explain the differentiation intellectually. X may still have difficulties being convinced, but this is not an exercise in how to listen with empathy to a person in pain.

B) Participant one, the person practicing how to explain a Key Differentiation, perhaps wants to also practice empathy. In that case guess briefly on needs and then resume explaining the differentiation. If you have decided on a limited time you may start with 1-2 minutes and thereafter, if you find a Key Differentiation of special interest you may want to use 10 minutes with the "opposing" participant to give clarity.

Exercise - Meet a Curious Sceptic

Purpose of activity:
To explore how knowledge around Key Differentiations can be used when connecting in ways that maintain connection and contribute to clarity.

Variation if you are on your own practicing:
Choose one of the sentences below and one of the 42 Key Differentiations (page X). Write an answer to the person saying the sentence, and continue writing a dialogue around the differentiation in question. Repeat with as many sentences as you find meaningful.

Variation for groups:
- Step 1: Divide participants into small groups; 3-5 people.
- Step 2: One participant plays "person A" and reads one of the sentences below out loud to one or more people in the small group. The same person can play A during the whole exercise or the role can alter between the group members.

Imagine that A is interested in understanding how the NVC principles can be used in the context in question. Even if A is skeptical or questioning he/she is not in pain, just genuinely curious. Allow yourself to take a minute or two to choose some of the Key Differentiations to use in a clarifying conversation with A.

- Step 3: Ask all group members to tell which Key Differentiations they think may contribute to clarity and understanding for A.

Step 4: Ask other groups to respond to A.

Variation of the exercise:

Step 4: Start by listening with empathy, and guess a need (see Key Differentiation 16 page X to connect with what is behind the question A has. Remember that the purpose of the exercise is not primarily empathy.

Sentences:

You can use your own examples of sentences challenging to hear, and where clarity of the Key Differentiations could be of help.

1. When I guess what someone is feeling and needing, I make interpretations all the time. I'm confused as I thought the whole purpose was not to interpret.

2. Why don't we just ask what someone is feeling and needing? If we do, we don't have to grope in the dark.

3. If someone shouts at me, it scares me. If no one is shouting, I'm not scared. So, of course it's the shouting that causes my fear.

4. Being a manager I cannot always just make requests. Sometimes I simply have to tell people what to do!

5. You know, when I say ..."I feel manipulated!" it is a much better description of what is alive in me than any of the words from that NVC-list of feelings.

6. I find the four components so blunt and impractical. I can't talk to my friends like that.

7. Why are authorities something bad? You know, I like it when someone takes on responsibility and is master of the house.

8. If I always make requests, no one will ever do what I want. So, one must have the right to make demands!

9. *When I hear all this stuff about self-empathy, I feel sick! I can't stand feeling sorry for myself. I'd rather scold the person causing my pain.*

10. *You will be treated like a doormat if you just listen and listen. Sometimes you have to tell people to quit!*

List of Key Differentiations

1. "Observations" versus "evaluations".

2. "Thoughts" versus "feelings"

3. "Needs" versus "strategies".

4. "Vague requests" versus "clear, doable requests".

5. "To request what I do want" versus "to request what I do not want.

6. "Request" versus "demand".

7. "Classical Giraffe" versus "idiomatic Giraffe".

8. "Living Giraffe" versus "doing Giraffe".

9. "Honesty in Giraffe" versus "honesty in Jackal".

10. "Screaming in Jackal" versus "screaming in Giraffe".

11. "No in Jackal" versus "no in Giraffe".

12. "Saying 'I am sorry' in Giraffe" versus "saying 'I am sorry' in Jackal".

13. "Empathy focusing on content" versus "empathy focusing on process".

14. "Empathy focusing on needs" versus "empathy focusing on unmet needs".

15. "Stating" versus "guessing".

16. "Guessing intellectually" versus "guessing empathically".

17. "Sympathy" versus "empathy".

18. "Advice" versus "empathy".

19. "Listen with empathy" versus "consoling".

20. "Mourning" versus "giving up".

21. "Self-empathy" versus "dwelling on feelings".

22. "Self-empathy" versus "acting out your feelings".

23. "Systems based on domination" versus "systems based on needs".

24. "Power with" versus "power over".

25. "Fear of authorities" versus "respect for authorities".

26. "Obeying" versus "self-discipline".

27. "Protective use of force" versus "punitive use of force".

28. "Moralistic judgments" versus "value judgments".

29. "Punishments" versus "consequences".

30. "Weakness" versus "vulnerability".

31. "External motivation" versus "inner motivation".

32. "Freedom of choice" versus "dependence".

33. "Dependence or independence" versus "interdependence".

34. "Appreciation" versus "approval".

35. "Stimulus" versus "cause".

36. "Compromise" versus "shift".

37. "Acts that serve life" versus "acts that distance us from life".

38. "Demanding" versus "persisting".

39. "Love as a feeling" versus "love as a need".

40. "Natural" versus "habitual".

41. "Accomplish" versus "create".

42. "Open questions" versus "closed questions".

Your Key Differentiations

In this book, we have made an attempt to visualize differences between concepts frequently used in NVC. It has been a challenging journey to examine, work and rework formulations that we hope will contribute to clarity for you. We are aware that this is not a full coverage of the subject.

We will continue exploring Key Differentiations. We encourage you as well to make your own list of words and concepts that you meet in your daily life, or hear from others. Do as we have done – try to describe the difference between for example: "deserve" and "need".

We welcome you to share words and concepts from your list with us, so that we can continue to help others gain greater clarity. Our objective with this book is, above all, to enhance our ability to communicate with each other, thus creating a world where everyone's needs are of equal importance to all.

References

Eisler, Riane (1987), *Chalice and the blade*. Harper Collins.

Haidt, Jonathan (2006), *The Happiness Hypothesis. Finding Modern truth in Ancient Wisdom*. Basic Books.

Frank, Viktor E (1959), *Man's search for meaning*. BeaconPress.

Kohn, Alfie (1999), *Punished by Rewards, The Trouble with Gold Stars, Incentive Plans, A's, Praise, and Other Bribes*. Houghton Mifflin Company.

Larsson, Liv (2014), *Walk Your Talk*. Friare Liv.
- (2014), *The Power of Gratitude*. Friare Liv.
- (2012), *Anger Guilt and Shame, Reclaiming Power and Choice*.
- (2011), *A Helping Hand. Mediation with Nonviolent Communication*. Friare Liv.

Rosenberg, Marshall B. (2005), *Speak Peace in a world of conflict, What you say next will change your world*. PuddleDancer.
- (2003), *Getting Past the Pain Between Us*. PuddleDancer Press.
- (2003), *Life-Enriching Education, Nonviolent Communication Helps Schools Improve Performance, Reduce Conflict, and Enhance Relationships*. PuddleDancer Press.
- (2003), *Nonviolent Communication, A Language of Life, Create your Life, Your Relationships and your World in Harmony with Your Values*. Second edition. PuddleDancer Press.
- (2003), *We Can Work It Out*. PuddleDancer Press

Schmockler, Andrew Bard (1988), *Out of Weakness, Healing the Wounds that drive us to War*. Bantam Books.

Elektronic Sources

Wineman, Steven. Power Under, Trauma and Nonviolent Change. http://gis.net/~swineman/
http://utveckling.mastercoach.se

Houghton Mifflin Company.

www.friareliv.se
www.13steg.se
www.nonviolentcommunication.com

www.cnvc.org

Katarina **Hoffmann** was introduced to Nonviolent Communication (NVC) in 1994. She received her NVC-training from Marshall B. Rosenberg – the man behind NVC - and is a Certified Trainer by the Center for Nonviolent Communication. She gives workshops and coaches individuals and groups in personal development, mediation and conflict management. She has worked as a reviewer of translations of NVC literature. Katarina has so far co-written two books with Liv Larsson.

She has a background in behavioral science, and has for 15 years been teaching sociology at the University of Linköping and the College of Jönköping in Sweden. Her teaching focuses on information and communication.

She is especially interested in developing different educational methods – her own and others – to use for spreading NVC. She is currently working on a method called "13 steps to make a difference".

Connect with Katarina at: www.13steg.se

Liv **Larsson** began giving workshops in 1978. For more than 30 years she has taught, lectured and tried to "walk her talk". She has been a LDMC (Leadership and Management Development Course) instructor since 1992. She began using Nonviolent Communication in 1999 and has been Certified as a Trainer by the Center for Nonviolent Communication. She has been sharing NVC with groups, managers, UN-personnel, peace workers, staff at orphanages, mediators, theatre groups, doctors, teachers and many more, in Sweden, Europe and Asia. She has written several books on NVC (for details see the reference list above) and has translated many of Marshall B. Rosenberg's books into Swedish. Liv has so far co-written two books with Katarina Hoffmann. Her books are published by Friare Liv, a publishing company she and her partner Kay Rung started in 1992.

"When I ask myself about the difference between key concepts in NVC, I have often found that it contributes to new depths in my own personal development. Looking at the Key Differentiations has helped me make active choices and given me openness when connecting to others. It has also helped me to 'walk my talk' according to my values, as it works as a 'handrail' in challenging situations."

Connect with Liv at www.friareliv.se/eng or www.livlarsson.com

Vilhelm **Nilsson** loves pictures. He trained as an Illustrator and graphic designer in Paris, France, and has worked for more than ten years as a freelancer. For several years he has brainstormed together with Liv Larsson and Katarina Hoffmann to find ideas for the illustrations in this book. The work has been of special interest to him, as it has been a challenge for him, both in terms of illustration style and of how to clearly communicate valuable ideas, using pictures.

The approach that NVC is based on is fully in line with his own philosophy of life. He feels that it is an honor to be able to contribute and influece the world in this way.

Besides having designed the covers for several books published by Friare Liv, he has participated in many NVC trainings and mediation sessions. One can say that the pictures in this book come "straight from his heart".

Connect to Vilhelm at vilhelm@uppsalanaturbete.se

Books by The Author

The Power of Gratitude
By Liv Larsson

ISBN: 978-91-87489-23-5
176 pages

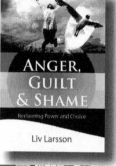

Anger, Guilt & Shame

Reciaiming Power and Choice
By Liv Larsson

ISBN: 978-91-979442-8-1
215 pages

Relationships
Freedom without distance
connection without control
By Liv Larsson

ISBN: 978-91-979442-0-5
69 pages

A helping hand
Mediation with Nonviolent
Communication
By Liv Larsson

ISBN: 978-91-976672-7-2
257 pages

For more information about Liv's Books:
www.livlarsson.com

37732088R00124

Made in the USA
Lexington, KY
01 May 2019